I'LL SING 'TIL THE DAY I DIE

I'll Sing
'Til the Day I Die

Conversations with Tyendinaga Elders

Beth Brant

McGilligan Books

CANADIAN CATALOGUING IN PUBLICATION DATA
Brant, Beth, 1941 —
    I'll sing til the day I die : conversations with Tyendinaga elders
ISBN 0-9698064-2-6
1. Mohawk Indian — History. 2. Mohawk Indians — Biography. 3. Tyendinaga
Indian Reserve (Ont.) — Biography. 4. Tyendinaga Indian Reserve (Ont.) —
History. 5. Indians of North America — Ontario — Tyendinaga — History. 6.
Indians of North America — Ontario — Tyendinaga — History. I. Title.
E99.M8B7 1995 971.3'585 C95-931928-X

Copy editor: Sandra Laronde
Transcription: Wiesia Kolasinska
Cover design: Jacqueline Rabazo Lopez
Layout: Heather Guylar
Author Photo: Amy Gottlieb

With thanks to the Elders for supplying the photographs, and to
Karen Lewis for making the photographs available for use in the this book.

Printed and bound in Canada.

Contents

Introduction

When asked to be Writer-In-Residence at Ka:nhiote Library at Tyendinaga, I was overjoyed. To be able to come "home" for a period of six months, to live and work among my people and to walk upon the land of my family and ancestors, was a gift containing many blessings.

I set up house at the Elder's Lodge on Bayshore Road thanks to the beforehand work of cousin Bob Lambert. I am grateful to "cousint" for taking the time to investigate the possibility of living there and for easing the transition.

As Denise and I drove up to the Lodge in May of 1993 in my daughter Jenn's pick-up truck filled with odd bits of furniture, curtains my mom had made, the sheets, towels, clothes and assorted things a person might need for half a year's stay, I felt complete. My new home overlooked the cemetary where my dear father's ashes are buried. I could walk up the hill and converse with him at any time. I could wander among the headstones and see the names of my relatives and know that everything is circular in this life. I was home.

Later that day, Denise and I took a drive through the Territory and we chanced upon a rookery coming to life with Blue Herons. They were building their nests again, bringing their unique beauty and spirit, returning to *their* home. It was a sign to me that this residency would be filled with new growth and wonder.

There are so many to thank. Jan Hill, for the loan of dishes, pots and pans, for her laughter, for her insight into Tyendinaga, and for her work on behalf of the returning of traditional thought and culture to our land. Karen Lewis, librarian at Ka:nhiote, for her hard work on behalf of literacy, books, culture; for the good times we had laughing and talking, for the invitation to return to the place that made *me* possible. My thanks to the Library Board, who had great patience with the duration of time it took to make this book possible.

Wiesia Kolasinska of Lyndhurst, Ontario, transcribed the tapes into text, and I never could have begun the process of editing without her initial work. Due to a faulty tape recorder, some of the tapes were very garbled, and Wiesia valiantly laboured to get every word. Thank you Wiesia.

Thanks also to Ann Decter of McGilligan Books who never got ruffled at the delays, whose phone calls were *gentle* reminders of deadlines, who always respected the fact that this book is a Tyendinaga project.

With all my heart, I thank the Elders who agreed to talk to me. After the initial shyness and the establishment, by some, of just *which* Brant I was ("oh, you're related to Alec, Tom, George, Benson, Mark, Elijah, Herbert, Enos; the Brant boys. Oh, your Grandma was a Powless, that must have been Maggie"), we were ready to go. They opened up their homes and their lives to me. I drank many cups of tea and coffee, ate many treats (especially Aunt Helen's raisin cookies) laughed with them, and cried my own tears at the sorrows expressed by them. I feel privileged to have been in their presence.

Through the transcribed text, my own notes, and my memory, I tried to reconstruct the stories that were given so generously. If something was left out, I apologise. In editing, I wanted to convey the sense of orality and how Tyendinaga Mohawks have always recorded the way things are and used to be. Through Elders' stories, we are given lessons in how to go about our lives in the best way we know how; values and tradition are imparted, warnings are given in the gentle and commanding presence of these voices.

Tyendinaga Elders have always been hard workers. Farming, factory work, domestic labour, migrant work during season, giving birth to and raising children; all these while contending with the outsiders' racism and misconceptions about our people. While talking with the Elders, I was stuck by the fear and worry that many expressed, in the loss of what is considered an inherent Mohawk trait — independence and self-sufficiency. Some expressed a contempt and anger towards government interference. Some worried that we were becoming too involved with the whiteman's way of doing things. All were concerned with the idea of what constitutes community — working as one to strengthen our people.

It is my hope that the younger citizens of Tyendinaga will read this book and learn, not just of a time long ago, but of the strength, endurance and dignity that has always been a hallmark of Tyendinaga people. That we continue on the path they worked so hard to establish for us.

Six months of my life were spent with Heron, Elders, relatives, ancestors, and lessons. I only hope that my small part in the making of this book is worthy of all that I was given in my beautiful homeland.

Nia:wen.

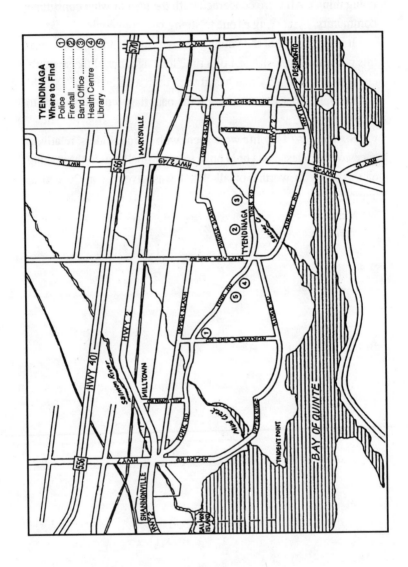

TYENDINAGA
Where to Find

Police .... ①
Firehall .... ②
Band Office .... ③
Health Centre .. ④
Library .... ⑤

Ka:nhiote

While working as librarian for Tyendinaga Territory, I had a desire to capture the oral histories of our people here; to record their memories of growing up and how they made their way in the world. There is not a great deal written about Tyendinaga, nothing that comes from the people and tells of our daily lives.

A happy chance of fate brought Beth Brant to us when she came to read her works as part of library programming. Some months later the mail brought the Library Project Grants announcements which included one for a Writer-In-Residence. This seemed like a marvellous opportunity and immediately brought Beth to mind. After talking to her about a residency, and discussion with the Ka:nhiote Library Board, we decided to apply for a grant. Our chairperson, Jan Hill, wrote the proposal. We were fortunate to be chosen and Beth began a six month residency.

This book is truly a collaboration of the people of Tyendinaga, from the idea, to the proposal, to the telling and collecting of stories.

Much thanks to our people who graciously shared their stories. Some of them have passed on or are seriously ill, and this book is a lasting testament to their lives. Nia:wen kiwahi.

Much thanks to Beth Brant who persisted in contacting people, collected the stories, had the tapes transcribed, and searched for a publisher. Nia:wen kiwahi.

Thanks to Karonhyontyeh who took time from his busy schedule to write a short history of Tyendinaga. Nia:wen kiwahi.

This would not have been possible without the support of the people of Ontario through the Ministry of Culture, Tourism and Recreation, who funded the Library Project Grant. Nia:wen kiwahi.

Karen Lewis, Librarian, Ka:nhiote Library

Tracing the Roots

There have been several accounts of written history about the Mohawks of the Bay of Quinte. However, the problems with many of the historical analyses are European influences and ignorance of Iroquois custom and culture.

Some people naively depict the history of the Iroquois (of which the Mohawks are one of the Confederate Nations) as evolving from white explorers accounts of it. Iroquoian history is recorded differently than that of the whiteman, and it is a system that has worked quite well for us.

Our history evolves from a time long ago, before the adversity of contact. Once there was war between many Aboriginal Nations of Turtle Island. As it is told, The Peacemaker brought five of those warring Nations together as one. They cast their weapons of war beneath the Great Tree of Peace, and vowed to never wage war amongst themselves. These allied Nations promised to uphold the constitution of the Five Nations Confederacy, (later, Six Nations, with the adoption of the Tuscarora) known as *Kaianerenko':wa*, or the Great Law of Peace. While united, no other peoples would match the power of the Confederacy.

This is our history as passed down from generation to generation by the Elders. Our Elders are walking history books. They have acquired lifetimes of knowledge during their stay on Mother Earth. Although there may be no specific dates attached, nor Carbon-14 dating to support the accounts of this verbal history, it is the way we have recorded our story since our existence — long before Columbus, or the coming of Cartier.

However, the story of the Mohawks of the Bay of Quinte unfolds much later in written history, in the late 18th century — the period of the American Revolution. At that time there were two major Mohawk settlements, one at Fort Hunter and the other at Canajoharie. The ancient homeland of the Mohawk, the Mohawk Valley in present-day New York State, became the whiteman's battlefield during this war. The Mohawk and other Iroquoian Nations declared neutrality, despite being courted by both the rebels and the British in their attempts to gain military advantage. It was the whiteman's war.

The position of neutrality by the Iroquois was in honour of an agreement made with the Europeans many years before, known to the Iroquois as the *Kuswhenta* or Two Row Wampum. Under this contract, a wampum belt was made to officially record this agreement. The belt symbolizes the conditions under which the Iroquois welcomed the Europeans to this land. The two separate rows on the belt show the paths of two boats on the same river. One path being for the Europeans, their laws and customs; and the other path being for the *Onkwehonweh*, the laws and customs and way of life. Under this agreement they shall travel side by side, but in their own boats, and neither will try to steer the other's vessel or interfere with the internal affairs of the other.

After massive bloodshed and chaos, some influenced Warriors of the Mohawks and other affiliated Nations, joined in the fight as allies of the British in attempts to secure their homeland. After seven years of fighting, the Revolution came to an end with the signing of the Treaty of Paris. No provision was made to include the Mohawk or other Iroquoian Nations. A number of Fort Hunter Mohawks, who fought alongside the British, abandoned their homeland in the Mohawk Valley and took refuge in Canada at Fort Lachine, Quebec. The British assured their Mohawk allies (not subjects as conjectured by the Crown) that they would be compensated for the losses, and land would be set aside for them. Similar promises were made by the Americans. These promises were broken, resulting in the burning of Mohawk villages after the revolution, known to our people as the Burnt Earth Campaign.

The six years the "Loyalist Mohawks" spent at Lachine were ones of hardship and disease. The Mohawks were anxious to sow their seed corn and other crops, rather than depend on the food supplies doled out to them at Fort Lachine. Under the leadership of Captain John Deserontyon, approximately twenty Mohawk families embarked on a voyage to search for suitable agricultural lands. On May 22, 1784, they landed on the east shores of the Bay of Kente, presently known as the Bay of Quinte. As a show of loyalty and appreciation, on April 1, 1793, a tract of land measuring one hundred and fifty square miles was officially granted to the Six Nations peoples by British Lieutenant Governor John Graves Simcoe, on the shores of the Bay of Quinte, between the present locations of Napanee and Belleville. The tract of land was later called *Tyendinaga*, after another Mohawk leader, Captain Joseph Brant, who settled with a larger group of Iroquois at Grand River, near Brantford, Ontario. Today, a number of the descendents of the Fort Hunter Mohawks are known as the Mohawks of the Bay of Quinte.

Today, with a membership of over five-thousand people (approximately two-thousand on Territory), Tyendinaga is one of the most progressive Aboriginal communities in Canada. But with progress came sacrifice and loss. Many of the Mohawks of the Bay of Quinte are retracing the footsteps of those who came before us, in order to restore the language, laws and culture as set down by The Peacemaker. After years of oppression, deprivation and cultural loss, it is difficult to trace the roots of the Great Tree of Peace. But, as our Elders teach us, everything has a cycle — life, Mother Earth, the creatures, *and* the Mohawks of the Bay of Quinte.

Nia:wen

Karonhyontyeh

Eva Maracle, 1896 –

Well, there was five boys and two girls and there's just two

left now. Wilbur and I are the only ones left. I've always

enjoyed life you know, but right now, you know I'm alone, and

I can go where I want to go and stay as long as I want to.

Come and go, mingle with the people here at the Elder's

Lodge. I don't have to worry about shovelling snow or

anything like that. I really, really love it here. I enjoy life now.

When I was a child, our house, it was one big room, and one big room upstairs, and everybody had a bed, there was beds here and there and all over. Then in later years, oh, I think I might have been around ten, yeah around ten years old, my dad built a partition up in the big room. And the boys used to sleep in one part and the girls in another. That's how we lived you know. No electricity, no TV, no radio or no telephone or anything like that. Kerosene lamps, not like they have today.

I've seen an awful lot of change in this reserve since I was little. Everything has changed, even the people. Changed for the worse, I'll tell you the reason why. Our family, all the folks used to help one another. We all used to help each other. Of course, there was no hospitalization either at that time. And when they was ill, if there was any illness, no matter what end of the Reserve they lived, the people would take turns. Oh, I remember my mother and my aunt, they had to walk too, unless they wanted to hitch up the buggy, but they never did, they always walked. And they started out maybe after supper, and they'd go out and stay with these people, so the others could have a rest. And they'd stay all night long, come home about four or five in the morning. All the people came to help you. And you did the same. In the fall, they'd come and help you do the plowing, draw in your hay. And they used to grow a lot of corn in them days. And of course they'd bring it in, you know, and then they'd have husking bees. We'd husk the corn and hang it up to dry. And that's the way they lived. We were all poor, but we helped one another. And I'm sad that we don't help one another any more like that.

The school part of it, we had to walk, wade in the snow. You should have seen the winters we used to have. You wouldn't believe it. And it would start in November, right up until around March or April. Then it would start to break. Oh dear, cold - twenty-four, twenty-five below for weeks at a time, weeks at a time. We had these

Eva Maracle

old-fashioned wood stoves, you know. They were different sizes and believe you me, they really threw the heat, because they were cast iron. They used to burn hardwood, and you know that really throws the heat. And that would heat everything. Of course, the house wouldn't be all that warm in the morning. It was cold! And snow! Sometimes you couldn't see, only maybe this much of the roofs of the houses. All you could see when you got up in the morning is smoke, going way up there. All over, you look and see smoke going up, up the chimney, out in the air.

And as far as roads, there was no roads. They just had to go whichever way the horses could get through. Over the fences, whatever. And it would get crusty, and there'd be great big snow-banks, huge snowbanks. We lived up there on York Road, we lived on a little hill, and there'd be snowbanks there. And at night, there'd be moonlight and then you'd see the snow glittering. You don't get moonlight like that anymore. Oh, it was all so lovely to see that moonlight on the snow. You could hear horses coming, the sound would carry so far. And that's how we had to live. We had no entertainment, we made our own entertainment. The kids, the neighbour kids, we had different games we played. Oh, sometimes we'd have a taffy pull, what they called a taffy pull. The only way it could harden was to put it out on the clean snow till we could cut it and eat it. And sometimes we'd crack hickory nuts. We did a lot of laughing.

Mom and Dad worked the farm. Well, at 8 o'clock at night my mother would say, "Bar's closed now." And we knew what that meant, "Shut up and go to bed!" It must have been hard on her to have seven noisy kids. Dad used to work at the smelter too. There used to be ore boats come in, iron ore boats come in the Bay. The men used to go down there and unload the boats for a dollar a day, twelve hours a day. And that was a lot of money at that time, because you could buy six quart-boxes of strawberries for a quarter, and ten cents a dozen for eggs. And ten cents for a loaf of bread. So you see, what can you buy for ten cents today? Nothing, not even a candy.

My mother and dad spoke Mohawk. But I'll tell you something, in my generation we were not allowed to say one word of Mohawk language. If you did, you got the strap. And that was the government did that. So this is why we don't understand the Mohawk language, and that's a shame. Of course, they're starting to have classes, teaching the children and they have adult classes. I learned it there. The grown-ups always spoke the language to one another, and they did to us kids until we went to school, and that's what happened. And then they were afraid to talk to the children in Mohawk, for fear of what might happen. They didn't know what might happen, if maybe the kids would be taken away, or punished. That was really, really bad. On other Reserves, Indian kids talk their language. But here, the government just took over and said we couldn't talk it no more. There was always a stool pigeon at school, "Oh, that so and so is talking Mohawk out there." Well, you got called in and the stool pigeon got the chocolate bar and you got the strap. You didn't dare say one word in Mohawk, not one word.

Another thing that happened too, is that there's been a lot intermarriage on the Reserve. And don't you know that some of those white women and the Native men didn't want the women to get their status back in '85. That makes me mad! And the things that go on today are terrible. We didn't have those things like child molesting. The government just interfered with us and all these bad things happened. It seems like we forgot how to take care of one another. That's the government's fault.

Well, I went up to 8th grade. I wanted to go to high school, but my parents couldn't afford to buy my books. Not like today, everything's given to them. They're bussed to school, they're getting a good education. And that's good, but in them days, the Native people had to fight for their survival. Ever since the Europeans came over here, it's fight, fight and still fighting for survival. It just makes me sick to hear these people from Europe say that *we're* immigrants, come over from the Bering Strait or something like that. Why, we've always been here, forever and ever. And they take our good land and they're still trying to take it. The guy that landed here, he thought he was in India! And they think that he was the one that discovered North America, but it was already occupied when he came here. I heard this professor from Montreal on TV, and he said that the French people were here before the Indians were! Boy, if I could've talked back to him I'd say, ''Hey man, don't you know that when the French people came over here, the Indian people helped them survive and how to make a living?'' So this is how ungrateful those people are. We feed them, and then they shoot at us like at Oka.

When I finished grade eight I went to work. My sister and I, we both worked in Belleville in a hotel. I don't know how long we

Eva Maracle

worked there, but we worked a long time. Then we quit there and the both of us went to Toronto. I was only about sixteen, her and I went to Toronto and we didn't know anybody up there. Of course, Toronto wasn't like it is today, it was different. We each got a job not too far apart. She got a job with a banker, like a live-in maid, and I got a job with two old maids. I don't know how many years I stayed with them. I quit there and I came home for a while, then I went back to Toronto and I got a job in the King Edward Hotel. I worked there as a maid, that's all I could do.

When we were doing housework, we each got about $8 a month. But you could do a lot with that at the time. We used to send half our money home to mother because there was still younger kids at home. We would have enough money for ourselves, to buy clothes, to go see a show, vaudeville shows. My sister and I had fun. We used to visit one another at night because we only lived a few blocks apart, and we weren't afraid to go out on the street at night. You'd never go out alone today. No way! Then it was all free, now it's nothing but a rat race up there. I didn't have any problems because I'm Native, but I was one of the lucky ones. Oh, I used to clean the house and dust and get the meals. And that's where I learned to cook! My sister's employer was good to her too. We were lucky. I enjoyed it. After my children got to be teenagers, then I went back out to do housework.

After I went back to Toronto to work at the King Edward, there was about twelve of us girls. It was a huge hotel and we each had so many rooms to do. We had a little dining room on the third floor, a dining room for the chambermaids. At night, we had a lot of fun, just visiting back and forth. We'd talk and joke. So anyway, one of the girls one night, she said, "Let's go to the fortune teller. I know one. Who wants to go?" So most of us went and the fortune teller described the man I was going to marry. And I thought, how was I going to meet a Native fellow, I don't know anybody. It wasn't too long after that, my cousin in Hamilton was getting married and I got the time off to go. And at the wedding, this is where I met my husband. He was from here, but they moved away to Hamilton. So I met him again, and I guess the fortune teller was right! I was twenty-four when we got married. We were married sixty-four years when he died.

During World War 1, I worked at a munitions factory in Toronto. I got the same wages as the white folks. I did the same work they did. We worked nights. I had to solder the heads on the shells. These great big machines cut steel and you had to put your foot on the pedal to bring it down to punch the strips. You had to wear gloves because the steel was sharp. It was hard work and so was the soldering.

War is terrible. In the Second World War, my oldest son went overseas, and he was only seventeen. He was in that Dieppe raid and got some shrapnel and he was taken prisoner. He went over with three buddies his age, and the others got killed. He was taken prisoner. When I got the telegram saying he was missing, I was standing between the fridge and the stove. My daughter come in and read the telegram, and my legs just gave way and I slid to the floor. It was almost two months after that, I got a second telegram saying he was a prisoner of war. And he spent three years over there, three birthdays, until they were freed. I knew he wasn't being treated right over there. He didn't like to talk about it too much after he come back. It was, oh more than year, then he began to open up. One day he told me that they were chained in the camp, from the wrist to the ankle. He said one morning they were supposed to be taken out to be shot. They took them all out, up on this hill. They took them up there and he doesn't know what happened, but they didn't die that day. He said some of the guards was really rotten, so mean. I never, never thought there would be another war so soon after the first one. Oh yeah, them wars are terrible, you know. All those head men want these wars and they can just sit back and send the young boys to get killed. I hate wars.

After John and I got married we stayed with my parents. Then we stayed with his folks, they had a big house and gave us a room. John used to go across the Bay, on the ice, and clear a man's woods. Cut the wood down, and that's what he did in the wintertime. He'd sell the wood and that's how we made a little bit of money. When that was finished, they started to build No.2 highway through the

Reserve. They had a gravel pit back of my father's place and they used to get the gravel there and that's where my husband worked until that was finished.

And then there was no more work, no welfare, no nothing, no work. So John hitch-hiked - I had a brother in Oshawa - so he hitch-hiked to Oshawa. When he got there it was around midnight and he went to my brother and I guess he wakened them up. They opened a window and wanted to know who was there and John told them. My brother says, "Well, we don't have any room." Oh, I will never forget that. It was hard to forgive him for that. Then John hitch-hiked to Hamilton, he knew some people there, and he got a job with a moving company. People he knew said we could stay with them for a while, so I went up there with the kids. Then he got laid off and went to Windsor and got a job across the river in Detroit. Oh, he worked hard for us. We found a house to rent and we stayed in Windsor for years.

All my children were born at home. We had a midwife, a cousin to my mother. She was good. She stayed right there with you for five days until everything was okay again. All of us were born in the house, my Grandmother was midwife. I think they're better than the doctors. They just knew everything to do. And it seemed like you had less pain with the midwife there. I wonder why they don't have many midwives anymore. Probably the government again, interfering where they're not wanted.

So we came back here when my dad was sick. We took care of him for years, and then my mother. We lived in Deseronto, then I moved to the Lodge. I started singing with the Mohawk singers in 1964, right from the beginning. We translated some of the English hymns into Mohawk. And we sang them and travelled all over and even made records! When the Queen was here in '84, my daughter and I worked hard, beading and sewing to get our outfits done to sing for the Queen. She was supposed to come in July, and we worked and worked, then after we got them all ready, we got word she wasn't coming until September! She wanted to hear "O Canada" in Mohawk, and we had to get busy and translate that into Mohawk.

Oh my, we have fun when we travel. Every place we've gone,

we get a good reception. But here on Reserve, some of the people don't think we should sing. Some people are ashamed of their Nationality, of Mohawk. And some people think we shouldn't be singing the Christian songs. But I like to sing and I'll sing till the day I die.

Ike Hill, 1900 –

I was born on this land. The old man was born here. My grandfather was born here. There's more than twice the houses now. Oh boy, there is large houses too. Not like the old days. But, I tore the old house down and built this one in '52. Yeah, I put up the barn first, and then the hen coop was set, and the pig pen and then the corn crib. Then I put up the house! I quit farming in '75. Oh, I used to have a lot of horses. I sold a hundred and thirty-eight head of horses since '75. And I went down to the shore and I cleaned that up and you should see that shore now. Boy, it's wonderful. I left all the trees, you know. I got willows all the way down to shore, and there's sand — the children like to go swimming there.

Oh man, we had to work when I was a kid. I didn't talk English then, we talked Mohawk. I was brought up in Mohawk. When I went to school, I didn't understand a word. I didn't know 'yes' or 'no.' But you know, I finished public school. The teacher used to like me because I had a nice mother and she was a good cook. The teacher used to come home with me at night, me and my sister, and have supper at our place. Oh yeah. But that was my step-mother. My own mother died when I was ten months old. You know, that's why I hate to see anybody call their mother down, oh that bothers me, that hurts

Ike Hill

me. I'd give all I own to have a mother. Yeah. I put her up a tombstone after I got big enough. There was six of us. But my step-mother was a wonderful woman too. She made our overalls and made our coats. She made our caps. Yeah. Oh, she was a nice woman. That was quite a while ago. Doesn't seem so long though, not to me. No. I'm, I'll soon be ninety-three, yeah. And these days, I have a couple of cooks come in and a washwoman comes every other Friday. She comes in and takes all my clothes. They all like to come here, yes they do. And when they come, they fix my bed and everything else. And when they don't come I do it myself.

I learned a lot in school, and we didn't learn the whole world, you know, just the stuff in Canada here. I think in high school you learn a whole lot. After I got to talk English...they never talked English at home. They all talked Mohawk. Yeah, my mother and father, they never spoke...awful broken, you know. But they could get along with other people, because they was trying to get along too, and they'd do anything to help friends too. Oh, it was a wonderful life, yeah.

So, I went away to work, not quite four years, making bathtubs. There was a bunch of us Native guys making bathtubs. You know, cook them and one thing and another. I used to be on the grinder, after they come out of the kiln, I smoothed them all up. After I got in, I worked heating the enamels, that was a better job, but hot in the summertime. They'd have to heat the bathtub red-hot when they put that stuff on. Then it was too hot to move. You just had to take what they give you in them days. You better not be jumping around from job to job because you'd never learn nothing too much. I got that from the old man. And do you know something, I got to see spider-climbers, sky-walkers, they work on bridges. Sometimes they build bridges sixty, seventy stories high. And they jump around there just like they was playing. I wouldn't take a thousand dollars an hour for that! That's the truth. I like to climb around little houses and barns, but I ain't gonna go climb them bridges. But they come to the Mohawks and get advice on how to build bridges. Yeah. The Mohawks make the best sky-walkers.

I miss my Missus. She was quite a worker, too. She used to go out and feed me at three o'clock in the afternoon. And in the morning too. I'd see her coming across the fields with the basket. I think that basket's outside, I use it for my kindling. I still burn a stove. I've a notion to get another heater, one of them oil heaters, you know. I tried to save the Missus. I was so glad when she was coming home from the open-heart surgery. God, I thought her dead. We only used this here wheelchair a little while. She had both legs cut off, yeah. She had a hard one. And that all come, one right after the other. And then afterwards I had a stroke. Now I'm no damn good! Just sit around. I can sit on a tractor though. I can work. Long as I have lots of power under me! But I had my wife's clothes up there in the attic and I told my girls, "Please do something with them, I can't look at them." Yeah, I miss her, and that's been a long time ago.

That machine you're using, it records everything I say? Well, that's the way to do it. I like that machine. So much change around here. I remember the first thrashing machine. Yeah, I remember the first traction engine. We had a steam engine. Yeah, that's a long time ago. Now they have gasoline engines and...young people won't believe, but I tell them. We used to do everything by hand and with horses. Cut grain with a sickle. Yeah, and corn too. They had no machines like they got today. We used to use our hands, you know. Sure. Maybe it was better back then. They had a better time. We had nice neighbors. The people was nice. They worked together and everybody...some person would get sick or something, why everybody would come and help you out. Yeah. Women getting sick having kids, there was always a gang of women to help with that. They hated the doctor, 'cause the doctor would just be in the way. And they'd do a lot better themselves. We knew the kinds of medicine to use. That's not like that now. You have to go to the hospital, stick you in the hospital and the next day send you home. Whether you get better or not, who cares. That's what it is today. We were all born at home and so was all my kids, but one, and we had more trouble with him than...he had more doctors and was sicklike. That's what happened when you're not born at home. How come nobody gets born at home anymore? We had wished for a boy and a girl, and we ended up with ten. Five boys and five girls. Whether you believe it or not, that's true. I have grandchildren, great-grandchildren. Pure bred Indians.

I was twenty-eight when I got married. Yeah, I had a nice bunch of money when I got married. I used to work out, you know, before I was married. And yeah, I had a nice bunch of money and we had so much to buy like tables, stove, cupboard, and dishes and pans. Boy, before I knew, I was broke! I had to farm like hell then! Yeah, the old man made me stay home. I got a job in Port Hope and he went up there and he made me come home and start plowing. He says, "I'm getting too old. I can't plow and you have to come home. After all the place is yours when I'm through with it." And he says, "You just have to come home with me." So I quit and come home. By golly, you take boys today, they won't come home with you. What I had to do, go home and start farming. Why didn't you work out, but there was no work! That's why we had to farm. Just like the old song the old people, I used to hear them say, "If I only had a horse and a cow and a plow, I'd get along somehow." And that was the end of that song. There was six of us, but I had to quit my job and go home. But that was the way it was then. But I had a nice bit of money to get married with.

I used to do a bit of hunting. I used to go up there with the Algonquins, they used to own Algonquin Park. They kicked them all out of there and put them on the reserve. And they made a great big park out of their land. Algonquins, yeah, I used to go hunting with them. Get some deer, maybe a moose. There was bears there too. So many animals, they used to run right at you, like they knew we were hunting them. Never seen anything like it. And them Algonquins treated their animals real special like. Almost like a brother. Yeah, they took away the land, and now there's a big park up there, and I hear that the Algonquins are trying to get the land back. But that's the way they do...take away the land, and put the people on reserves.

Our reserve is getting small. Filling it up with new houses. There won't be any land left. Yeah. I did a little hunting, I did some trapping. 'Rats. Muskrats. Oh, a guy from here, me and him went into partners, catching 'rats, selling them for five dollars straight. Boy, sometimes we'd catch anywheres from thirty-five to sixty-five 'rats a day. We used to skin them and hang them up every weekend the 'rat buyers would be going around. They used to like to come here because we used to catch a lot of 'rats. We were usually the best trappers on the reserve. Yeah. They used to like muskrat. We used to eat it ourselves. We'd take the hind legs, yeah that's all. We'd just cut them in two in their skins, you know, and take the scent out of them and cook them up. They was nice, oh yeah. We had big marshes here. In the spring as soon as it starts to open up, we'd set the traps, go out in the bog. But nobody traps anymore. Sometimes we got the odd mink or two. They was worth gold, but they were trickier than 'rats.

I never did any travelling, except maybe the Missus and I would go to Toronto for the Exhibition. I have a daughter up in B.C. I was up there. Went up there, first time I was on a plane. It was nice. It was nicer than a bus ride. We went to Toronto at the big airport, you know, where the big airport is in Toronto? We got off in Vancouver. And do you know how long it took us? Three hours! Well, that thing was up there the thousand...ten thousand feet. Yeah. I was going up, geez it's nice going up, go right through the clouds and everything. After we got up a certain distance, they tell us how high you are, you know, and then she straightened up and away she went. And then, she starts coming down, come down you know, and it starts shaking. Boy, that's hard on your nerves, and then when we got off the plane my ears was stuffed up. I could hardly hear. Just like when you go swimming and the water gets in your ears, you ever get that? That's what it felt like, after getting off this plane. I guess because we was on the plane so long, it wasn't because it was noisy. God, I was scared! We was all wondering what to do. But that's the farthest I ever been away from here. That's something, isn't it? Some folks from here travel all the time, but never learn a thing from it!

We just worked and worked, doing chores, maybe going to school. We had to do everything before we went to school, milking and one thing and another. Not like they're doing now. Some of them now, they're not up early enough to catch the bus. They don't know how to work. You know what's gonna happen? It's gonna be bad if everybody quits working. The white settlement is just as bad, maybe worse. A lot of them don't want to work. I don't know what's going to happen. Some of these young people say to me, "You're crazy to do work. What's the matter with you? Why don't you go out and have a good time?" I just laugh and shake my head, "What's wrong with work? I did it all my life, I ain't going to let a stroke stop me!"

But the school part, that was a bad time, sometimes. The agent that hired the teacher told them to make the kids quit talking Mohawk. Well, that's a pretty hard thing to do, but he says all you gotta do is give them a damned good licking anytimes they say something in Mohawk. He says they learn better. And so, that's what happened. All through my school days, if I just spoke one word of Mohawk, I'd get a licking. I got lots of lickings for talking our language. But today, the government is hiring people to get our language back. They're learning them how to talk Mohawk in school. Isn't that crazy, the way they used to be? And that didn't make the children learn any better.

I'd be home and all we'd speak is the language. And I went back to school and I didn't dare speak a word of Mohawk. But just the same, sometimes the words would get away from me, I'd say something and somebody would tell on me. Usually the white girls, you know. Not the boys, they wouldn't even give a damn, but the girls, they were squawkers. They'd squeal — he's talking Mohawk again. All right, the teacher says, I'll have to doctor him up. And she'd come along with the strap, just as hard as she could get, with a great wide strap. You had to hold your hands out and if you pulled them away and she hit her knees, oh boy, she'd hit you harder. I've seen her get me across the neck with the strap. Oh, that was rough. A lot of people don't believe that, but it's true. That's just as true as anything. Too bad. But that's the way they was hired — give 'em a licking if they talk Mohawk. If they say anything in Mohawk, give them a good licking. And that's just what she done. It's a dirty shame. That didn't make them stop. When they got home, they went right on talking Mohawk. It got so that you wondered if maybe the walls had ears, and you'd start talking English more at home. It's a dirty shame what they made us do.

I've been in school. I could have went to high school, but my dad didn't have the money to go on buses, we had to hire my board, stay in Belleville, and pay for my books. Now they furnish books for them, and they sleep right up until the bus comes to the door, and they get up and away they go, they're lacing their boots on the bus going to school. And the reason is...no chores. They made us work and they made us learn. Oh, some of them teachers was bad eggs! And the agent, well it wasn't all together his fault. The government told him to do that. You can blame the government for that. You gotta hire teachers, they said, and you gotta tell them to give a damn good licking if they didn't quit the Mohawk. Just forget about the Mohawk. And that's exactly what they done. All during my teaching, going to school. My old man used to get mad and go down there and give the teacher trouble, that didn't do no good. No. They'd just send the agent down to give the old man hell. And I got extra lickings at school. Oh, it was hard. But not all the teachers was like that one. I one time had me a nice teacher who used to come home with me and my sister. Such a terrible thing to be punished for speaking your language. I'll never forget it, no.

I brought up my kids right through the dirty thirties, yeah. Oh, that was a rough time. The old people, they was going around with canes with nails sticking out on the ends — they'd go along and they'd see a cigarette stub some place and they'd jab it, and put it in their pocket. They had a great big pocket full of tobacco. Sometimes they'd put it in a clay pipe and smoke it that way. Oh, I remember them days, them dirty thirties. But the missus and I managed to keep the kids fed. That was the thing having a farm. You could always have the seeds and grow your food, and we used to do the hunting or the trapping so we'd have meat. But them folks up there in the city, they didn't have nothing. Well, neither did we, but we was used to not having anything.

Oh, you know, I have lots of tunes. I used to be a fiddler, you know, and I learned to play those tunes just right. You got to play it just right, so that everybody will sing in tune. Yeah. And I used to step-dance, yeah. We had lots of dances. Oh, we had a lot of fun. Me and my missus used to have the first dance down at the Council House, or at people's houses. You see, we used to go around to people's houses and have get-togethers and dances. I don't think the people do that sort of thing anymore. Oh, it was great doings then. But maybe they didn't just take our language away…maybe they took away our having fun.

Susie Janes Lynch, 1902 –

If you want me to talk Indian, I will. I guess I'm the only one that talks Mohawk anymore around here. We were raised, all spoke Mohawk. We were lucky. After I got working around, that's where I learned English. My grandmother, I never heard her talk Mohawk till after she took sick, and then she talked Mohawk. I was surprised. I didn't think she could talk it, but she did. But I never talked English until after I started working out on my own. I was thirteen when I started working out.
'Cause we were poor.

My father, he was lazy and he kept telling my mother to keep me home and not go to school, so I could do the work. My mother said, "You can't go to school, you got to stay home and help with the work." I went to school a little, maybe a year all told. My father worked this place on shares, that's where we were living when they married me off. I was only sixteen. He was my first cousin. Oh, he was mean. He used to call me, even if I just talked to my brothers, I had a licking. Oh, I had quite a time, he used to pound me, oh, even if I just talked to my brothers. He even put me in jail one time. I don't remember what for, but oh, he was mean. Then I left him. We parted and I worked out doing housework and my mother used to babysit my children.

I worked for Andy Hill, milking cows, keeping house. I got paid a dollar a day. That was good pay. I worked in other places too. I stayed at my mother's. Then I had a home of my own, four or five acres, but after my children left me, I got rid of everything. I says, there's no use me working my head off when the children didn't want to help me. So I stayed with my mother until she passed away.

I had seven brothers and one sister. We were crowded and right from the time I could work, I had to work. I didn't have much fun. I couldn't hardly even go to school, I had to stay home and work. They told me I can't sit on my ass in that schoolroom, I had to work. I often wished I had more education than what I got. You know, I picked up a lot, reading newspapers, and I'd spell, spell, spell till I got that word. The teacher used to come down and get after the old folks for not sending me to school. And it didn't make any difference. I tried to get along the best I could.

My mother was a midwife and she made me go with her to birth the babies. And they said I was better than my mother! I says, how could that be? But I was good at that kind of work. I can look after Indian women real good. I didn't want to do that kind of work, I was forced into it, but they said I was better than my mother. Some of them couldn't pay me, and I says I gotta live, too, and take care of my children, maybe you want to get the doctor next time! But most of them paid me, in money or in food. We used to use Sweet Flag for the after pain. It healed the women right up. I always had quite a bit on hand, I'd get in the spring. I used to go and get it in the spring when the water is up. Use the root, pull them up and put them away for later. We used to steep the root and drink it when we got a cold too. Mother used Bloodroot and I think she had seven different herbs she'd use for the women. Oh, we practiced different things. I used to watch my mother, she'd go out and gather the herbs and put a paper down upstairs on the floor near the pipe and lay the roots there and dry them out. The women would come to her for all kinda things, even how not to get babies. I learned a lot from her.

Things has changed around here. I said the other day that soon we'll be living in the bush! Nobody burns wood anymore and there's lots of trees and bushes growing up. The bogeyman lives in the woods. My mother said that a man with no face lives in the bush. We called him the bogeyman, but he had another name. Was it

O-Face? He'd grab the bad children. He consorted with witches. There are changes here. Nobody speaks Indian any more. Maybe it was good I didn't get schooling or I might've lost my language too. It's a dirty shame how they've lost the language. I always said I'd never lose it, even though I married a white man once. That didn't make me turn white. I met him in Hamilton after I went up there to work. He was from Nova Scotia and we were only married five years and he died. I must have been too much for him! Isn't that crazy?

I like to make a person laugh. That's how it used to be with my mother. I'd go to a dance and see funny people and I'd go home and tell my mother and have her laughing. It's a good thing to make people laugh. But there wasn't much to laugh at when I was young. They say I took after my mother, but I'm not as big as she was. But I'm glad I didn't take after my father. He was lazy and good for nothing but making children! I didn't miss him a bit when he died. You know his father was a whiteman. Never acknowledged him as his son. So, him and his mother was left out and real poor. Maybe that's why my father was so mean.

I used to grow things — corn, beets, tomatoes. And squash and beans to go with the corn. You got to grow them together or it isn't any good. I was busy all the time, cultivating, hoeing, the soil was real good. We never put any of them fertilizers in it, it was just good on its own. I used to fish, catch mudcats and suckers. And when my brothers hunted, I was the one had to do the skinning and cleaning. Yes, I had to work, but it was the best for me. I learned how to work.

I was born with a veil over my face. They say them kind make the best doctors. And I guess I did make a good doctor to the Indian women. And some people said I was smart. Even the white people I cleaned house for thought I was pretty smart. Maybe they thought that Indians wasn't smart, and was surprised at how smart I was. Even though I didn't get any schooling. I had to learn English on my own. So, I guess that makes me smart! And I learned to read. Do you see that newspaper? I can read every word of it!

But my father was stingy and lazy. He wouldn't buy a loaf of bread! When I was caring for my mother, he'd just take the money and put it in his pocket and use it for drink. Oh, he set my children against me. And my mother just kept him and put up with him. Imagine! I says, I wouldn't do it. No man's that good that has to be clothed and fed by me. No! When I was small, we used to go to Burlington to pick berries and make money. And there was an old man there who gave me ten cents because he said I looked like a doll, I was so small. You know, my father wouldn't rest until he got that ten cents off of me. He just stuck it in his pocket. Ten cents! Oh, he never liked me. They used to come down here and get pickers for the berries. There was two houses for the pickers to live in. We'd pick the strawberries, the blueberries, raspberries and cherries. I never saw a cent of the money I made. My mother worked like a man, but my father was good for nothing. Oh, we were so poor. I think it might have been better if my father worked, but he didn't do nothing but make babies and run around with other women. Oh, my poor mother.

Do you believe in witches? Witches don't like it when you're doing good, when you're good. I don't know what wrong I've done them, but they bother me at night. They want people to be unhappy. They're jealous. Oh, my oldest son, the witches bothered him. He had two wounds in his leg. Two pieces of pins come out of his leg, above the knee. Oh, he used to suffer something awful! It was my father's aunt was doing it. See, they put needles and pins in your limbs so you hurt so bad. They were witches, oh, they'd talk so dirty in Mohawk, and plot bad things to do to people. I would hear them and tell my mother. She'd tell me to stay away from them. They bothered one woman for a long time, she lost her baby and buried it not far from the house. And the two aunts dug it up. Oh, they were devils. You could tell by their voice when they were talking witch talk. It would change, their voice, like something bad. Oh, they even put a worm in my mother's arm. She come over so sleepy and tired. Then the worm crawled out and my mother stepped on it, then burned it. Oh, there are still witches here, but they're not so cruel as those ones. They died and they must be having a hot time with the devil down there! Some used to say that I was a witch, because I did such hard work and always had some money and sent my children to school, and I knew the herbs, the medicines. But I just laugh at them that said that. If I was a witch, I would've put my father down long time ago. I would have freed my mother from him.

I haven't had such a good life. I had a lot of beatings. It's a wonder I'm so old, the way I used to be beat up. Oh, my first husband, my father owed him some money, so he married me off to him. Imagine! I was sold like a cord of wood. Yes, he was lazy too. Just beat me and run after women. I guess that's why there are circles around my eyes, he used to give me black eyes. That's what I was saying to my niece, that must be why it's dark under my eyes, cause I used to have black eyes all the time. I got so I didn't care if he killed me, but I'd fight him back. I picked up a skillet, you know those iron ones, and let him have it on the head. He had the gall to say, "We can't live like this, you hitting me." I says, "No, you ain't gonna pound on me no more. I've got a life just as well as you have." He was three times as old as me. That was my father's work. Just selling me like I was a cord of wood. Well, I've had a tough life. But I'm still here and no man ever got the best of me again. No.

Eileen Green, 1904 –

I had a baby brother, but he passed away when he was nine months old. My mother died and I was all alone. Dad and I went to live with Grandma and Grandpa Brant at the homestead. Dad farmed and did any kind of work. Grandpa was a funny man, but I liked him. He was better than Grandma; she was really hard to get along with! She used to holler at me quite a bit. But my dad would stop her. I don't know why she hollered. Maybe I didn't do enough work or something. I don't know. I was so young then, I didn't care! But I had to do all the dishes on the table and you know, there was a lot of them, with all the brothers living there. I lived there until I got married. That's what you did.

I learned how to quilt from Grandma, and how to sew and do all those things. I first entered the Fair when I was eighteen. I exhibited every year until about four years ago. Getting too old! But I quilted and worked. Sometimes I'd go to house parties, and danced, danced all night. And I'd just get my bed warm when Grandma started hollering at me to get up and do my work! But I loved to dance. Sometimes people would bring the fiddles and there would be music. It was fun. But oh, I didn't like getting up at six o'clock to start my chores!

I used to do housework in Belleville. I'd get a ride with someone and he'd drop me off close to the houses I was to clean. I had to dust and wash. Some of the people were nice. Others, well…

I didn't get to high school. I liked school and then I didn't. One of the teachers taught us how to square dance. But I just wanted to play, and anyway, I was needed at home. I had to wash the milk separator. I had to do that. Then all the dishes. Oh, I done all those, then I had to bake bread. Five or six loaves at a time. We used the hard yeast in the cakes, not like the dried stuff you use now. It was

Eileen Green

harder then. I still got hollered at by Grandma. But I lived through it.

My husband and I had a long courtship. I didn't get married till I was twenty-six. We got married in Kingston, because we didn't want any fuss. We didn't have a honeymoon. People didn't do that. You got married and you set up house and went to work. Not very romantic, eh?

We used to have quilting bees and then there'd be harvest time and the people would come and help. You'd get a big meal in the afternoon, but nobody got paid for the work. I don't know if anyone would do that now! What a shame.

I think I've probably made about a thousand quilts in my lifetime. That's a lot, isn't it? So many pretty patterns. Mohawk Trail, Drunkard's Patch, Berry Fall, Log Cabin, Star Quilts. I think I sewed them all. We used to quilt at the Seniors' Hall and do a bunch of them together.

We had to do everything on our own. That's the way it was. Not like today. I remember when Edie was going to school and she asked the Indian Agent if he could help with her schooling. But he said no, and Edie just had to tough it out herself. But she became a nurse, you know, and then worked in Ottawa. It would have been nice if he could have helped her. I think it's easier now to get an education. But we had to do it on our own. When they paved the street out front, they gave me some money for paving the property, but then I had to give some of it to the Indian agent. He probably kept it. But then they got rid of him, I don't remember his name. I guess the people got tired of him or thought he wasn't doing what he should have been doing!

We always had a garden. How else could we eat? Lots of berries and potato beans. We canned. Of course I learned to can from Grandma Brant! I don't know if there was any kind of work I didn't do around the homestead. I had my cousins as playmates and that was good. We had nice Christmases. It wasn't that bad. My dad was always good to me, and Grandpa was fun. Maybe Grandma was just tired of having all those grown men to take care of! But she could be nice sometimes. I was just interested in playing or dancing. I didn't want to do all those chores!

Yes, it was hard, especially during the Depression. Oh, that was such a bad time here. No work, so little to eat. It was a bad time. But we made it through, didn't we? I'd say I had a good life. I sit and

Eileen Green and parents

watch tv. I like the cooking shows. Edie does all the work and she calls me into kitchen to make the gravy! I still make green corn cake and a few things. I say to Edie that I get a lot of pointers from the cook shows, even though I don't do too much cooking anymore! I like to read the cookbooks. I guess you'd say I like food. Maybe it was a good thing that Grandma Brant made me learn so much!

Helen Brant Spencer, 1911 –

We were poor. There was five girls and three boys. And we lived right next door to the Eastern Mohawk school, which is now the Senior Citizens' Hall. So we were right near the school and this is where we went to school. My older sisters did housework, they were maids. My sister Lydia worked for the manager of the bank in Deseronto. When they went on their summer holiday, Lydia would go with them to take care of their three boys. I used to help out my Aunt Alicia when the thrashing time began. I'd help get the meals ready. I was pretty little then. But I passed grade eight and even went to Deseronto to the high school for a couple of years. Then I got married. I was nineteen. So you see, that was my life!

My grandfather was given a piece of land up along the Bay in Shannonville. And when he died, he gave the land to my mother. Mother wanted to go and settle on her piece of land, so they built a little shack up there and we moved there. But I didn't live there too long because I was getting older and then I got married. My husband was non-Native and was a cheesemaker. He worked for his brother, but in '31, the president of a cheese factory wanted Bert to take over this factory. So, away we went and I think we were there for seven years. Then we moved again, and it must have been a great place

Helen Brant Spencer

because this is when we produced a son in 1940. Then we bought the cheese factory in Shannonville and of course, we were there for fifty years, you see.

There weren't too many Native students at the high school. I think I went there mostly for fun! Because, I can remember one time, I loved to play ball, and I had to catch the bus to go to Shannonville. And this one day, I was busy up at bat or something, when the bus went right on by me. And here I was in Deseronto and I lived in Shannonville. I got a ride with Lesley Claus to his place, then I walked, and my, it was a long walk. Oh, it was an awful walk, it must have been five miles anyway. But the Native students were treated different from the white students. I don't like to say, it was so long ago, but we persevered.

My mother and father spoke Mohawk, but no, we didn't. And that's sad because we should know our own language. I can say a few words, but very few. When my father started school, and I'm sure this is true of your Grandfather too, when they first started school, they couldn't talk English. No, they couldn't talk English. So, you know we have been discriminated against. In my years I spent among non-Natives, I worked very hard so I wouldn't be called a "dirty, lazy Indian." Because, you know, that's what they used to say. And when I'd have the president of the cheese factory to dinner once in a while, his wife would say to other people, "You could eat off any one of her floors." Then some of them would come in after we got a baby and say, "Oh my, he's so clean." Why wouldn't he be?! I worked hard so nobody could say bad things about Indians. But why would anyone want to eat off of floors?!

So true

But anyway, back as little kids, like I say, we were poor and we weren't the only ones who were poor. You'd go out with not very good shoes and there wasn't money to buy all the things that kids have nowadays. And so, you were poor and you learned to cope, that's what we did. I wonder how people are coping now. There's unemployment insurance, and there's welfare, but are you learning to rely on your own devices? The women back then didn't seem to let anything bother them. They had these really big families and we'd be poor and somehow, they'd make do and see that we had enough to eat. My mother was so nice. She was a wonderful mother. She didn't have it easy. She lost her mother when she was just thirteen, then she had a step-mother, you see. No, she didn't have it easy, but she was so nice.

Every year there would be a Sunday School excursion. We'd get on a boat in Deseronto at 8 o'clock in the morning and it would get to 12 O'Clock Point at 12 o'clock! So many people would have their breakfast on the boat, then we'd have dinner at 12 O'Clock Point. Then we'd leave at 4 o'clock and get home at 8. People would come carrying trunks of food, because you see, by July, there would be good things from your garden. Well, we didn't carry a trunk, but we had a good time anyway. After a while, people had cars, and the boat stopped going. So there were two things we went to — the excursion and the Mohawk Fair. Our Uncle Levi Brant had a change purse filled with coins and he'd give us some pennies to spend at the Fair. He was a wonderful man. That change purse was so fascinating, it made a jingly noise when he took it out.

In those days my father worked for the Canada Cement Co. at Point Anne, so I was born there at home instead of the Reserve. There used to be a farm where they would hire men to look after the farm you see, and my father worked there too. He wasn't the only one, there was other people who did this kind of work. And they were paid a little bit for it. Well, anyway, this is where I was born. Today, on that property, is a beautiful mansion. But that isn't where I was born!

People had to take jobs that were available. You see, they weren't educated to hold better jobs, and to have skills that paid better money. Oh no, they took whatever jobs were available. And my father was so close to all his brothers. They all got along so well together, and they would tease each other. Your Grandfather was a great tease. They all loved to go fishing, and Uncle Enos had a car, and we all went fishing and Cousin Hazel and I got in the car you know. The men were out fishing in the boat, and Hazel started fiddling with this thing and that thing, and don't you know she got the car to go! She started it and there's this big roar out of the car. They were out in the boat and they heard it. Uncle Enos started waving his arms and finally she did something to make it stop. It's a good thing it didn't go into the Bay. But Uncle Enos wasn't mad. They just laughed. Hazel and I were so close, even closer than sisters. After I got married, Bert and I would go fishing, and in the spring he'd trap muskrat. We'd sell the skins to a man in Belleville. We'd keep the meat and give it to people who liked it. I ate a bit of it.

I got along very well with my in-laws. There was only one lady who didn't like the fact that I was Native. The rest of them thought an awful lot of me. So I didn't care what this one lady thought and none of the rest of them did either. When Bert and I were going together, this one lady said to Bert's mother, "Now you'll have to do something about this." She didn't want me in the family, no she didn't. But Bert's mother said, "Every one of my boys married who they liked and Bert can do the same." So, we got along fine.

I didn't have a profession or anything like that, but I think you learn quite a lot along the way of life. I learned to make cheese and I did all the books at the cheese factory. People used to come in and watch me forking the curds. I knew how to do it better than the men! So even though I didn't get a lot of education, I learned quite a bit. I had a happy childhood. Maybe poor people are kinder, I don't know. Maybe Native people are kinder, but there was a lot of kindness in my childhood. I think each one of us have a life to live and we make our own life. If we want to go forward, it's up to us to do that, not sit in a corner and feel sorry for yourself. You just do the best you can. I know we are discriminated against, but we have to keep going.

We had four schools on Reserve. I only remember having white teachers, but I heard of a Native teacher who taught here, and he got recalled. It seemed he was just teaching the kids how to dance! Well, that was something, wasn't it?! I remember hearing about a white woman who was going to teach here, but other people told her, "Oh, my goodness, you don't want to go there. They're savages and they're dirty and this and that." All kinds of mean things. But when she got here, she saw ever so many nice people, and knew we weren't savages.

I didn't think it was fair that I lost my status because I married a non-Native. Many Native men brought non-Native brides here and that was okay. So why wasn't it okay the other way around? So, we were given back our status you see, and one morning I went to the post office to get my mail, "Oh," I says, "just look at this. I've been a white woman for all these years, now I'm an Indian again." We all had a good laugh at the post office. When I went to Toronto for the Advisory Council on Seniors, I told them that I had a number and my number was C31! So, I always knew I was an Indian, they just didn't think I knew it!

I remember when Bishop Tutu came through our country and he said we have a Third World right here among our Native peoples. He was right! It's been so unfair. And when I think about those poor people at Davis Inlet, it's a crying shame. Those people were sent there and there wasn't anything there for them, no hunting or anything. And those other Inuit people, sent to such remote places. And nobody understands why they're angry and upset. At least on this Reserve, we have an Elder's Lodge and it's very nice. And we take care of our Elders here. When we went to the Seniors' Advisory in Toronto there were quite a few Native people there. And I learned about really bad conditions on some Reserves. It's so sad. But I met a wonderful woman there, a Native woman, Verna Johnston. I think Native women have kept the communities going. And I think I must get invited to these things because I have a big mouth! But you know, Mohawk women have never kept their mouths shut when there are important things to say. If it weren't for Native women, we never would've got our status back. The men would've just let it go along forever. You see, they didn't have anything to lose.

Ella Claus, 1912 –

I was born on the Six Nations Reserve. My parents were

Clayton and Mary Monture. I made that my home until I met

Les, and we married and moved to Tyendinaga. When my

parents were first married, they lived on a rented farm and

when I was nine months old, my father bought a little farm of a

hundred acres among the Cayuga people on the northeast end

of the Reserve. They lived right on the boundary and the

people, our neighbors, were the Longhouse people of the

Cayuga. So my playmates were the Cayuga children who

attended the Longhouse and we were the only people that went

to the Anglican church. But there was no…they didn't

discriminate against us. In fact, they were just wonderful

people.

    My father exchanged work with the men, haying and harvesting, and I played with the children and I learned to understand Cayuga and speak some of it. And they spoke English as well. I have nothing but admiration for those people. I learned a great deal from them. Sometimes we went to the Indian school together, mostly in the winter. My closest friends and families went to the berry farms, fruit farms around Niagara. They went in May and maybe didn't come back until late September because they worked picking fruit, or sowing and planting. But some of my friends were around all summer long, the younger ones especially. I have very happy memories of my childhood among these people.

I learned a lot of their beliefs by listening to my father talk with his neighbors at mealtime because my father was interested in the traditions, and so I listened in on the discussions and learned a lot about traditional beliefs. They never tried to impose their beliefs on us. I remember Mr. Johnson and Mr. Longboat saying, "Someday," (they called my father, his first name was Clayton, and they always called him Mr. Clayton) "Someday, Mr. Clayton, you will realize just how important it is to worship like we do, Mother Nature." In many ways they were right. They used to tease us. We drove horse and buggy and on Sundays when we were going to church, as we passed by various homes, they would be out working, chopping hay or stripping the grain, and if they were near the road, they would indicate they wanted to chat. My father would stop the horse and they would say, "Which way now, Mr. Clayton?" And dad would say, "Oh, we're going over here to church." They'd shake their heads and say, "You worship one day a week, we worship every day." Dad would say, "Well, I feel the same way, but I go on Sunday to give special thanks." Then we'd all laugh and go on our way.

I went to school on the reserve. Most of the teachers were non-Indian, but then they'd accept an Indian teacher if they had grade ten. My mother's brother was a teacher and he had grade ten. He taught for years and years, then the government said he had to requalify. He was fifty and maybe he could have gone back to school but he had a large family and a farm, so he retired. It was his son, Arnold, who became a chemist at Dupont. During World War II, when the Americans were developing the atomic bomb, Arnold worked on that. And he met with Dr. Einstein, but he didn't know what he was working on, didn't know until after the war. He wondered why it was sent to different parts of the United States to work in certain factories. It wasn't until after the war that he realized that he had helped. He was upset. His mother has a letter thanking him for his part, but he says it isn't anything to be proud of. Arnold at one time was interested in theology, and when he finished high school, he applied to the college in Toronto, Trinity College. I went with him for the interview. As soon as I saw him after the interview, just the way he moved and hung his head, I knew it didn't go well. He said, ''They told me that Indians never make good students.'' He wasn't encouraged at all. So he went to McMaster University and he got his B.A. He was a clever, clever man.

Then I went to the high school in Caledonia, on the border of the Reserve. There was a train that passed just at the edge of our farm and the train came by at a quarter to nine in the morning. And I caught the train to Caledonia and I would walk about a mile to the high school. I was always late, but my parents cleared it with the school and I got to go. Then, when I was sixteen, my father bought a little car, the first Ford that had a gearshift, and I got to drive that car to school. My, I thought I was something! My father gave me a dollar for gas. That did me five days, back and forth. He seemed to know just how much it would take. Sometimes my friends would chip in a dime here, a dime there, and we'd buy extra gas and go for a little ride!

Being a Native was hard at school, pretty hard. My high school days were not happy ones. I had no social contact with the people in town, but I didn't care, because all my friends were on reserve. I had no brothers or sisters, but I had close family, relatives, friends. There were a few of us Natives, so we stuck together. So, I wouldn't let the discrimination bother me. My parents really encouraged me to get an education. I did make two friends with non-Indian girls, and we still keep in touch. But I graduated in 1932 from grade thirteen, and in 1982 we had a fifty-year reunion. There were twenty-three that graduated and seventeen of us Natives and that was a great thing.

I had a lot of good advice from people I respected and trusted. My father's younger brother was a very well-known man and he made his name, he was known all over before he died. He said he had made it to the top as an Indian, he never denied his roots wherever he went. He always said he was proud to be a Mohawk Indian. He was the youngest in the family, he was big and husky like his older brothers. My father and his brothers and sisters finished grade eight, but then they had to go out and work. But the youngest one went to high school. And he told me that one day when he was walking home, he had to walk five miles to high school, he was picked up by a Baptist minister and given a ride. The man said, "Why do you force yourself to go to school through weather like this? What do you expect is going to come of this, you're only an Indian, you'll never get anywhere." And that made him all the more determined to finish his education and go somewhere. He went to Queen's in Kingston, even. And during the holidays he would come and work on my father's farm. I think my first recollection of him, I must have been four or five…was sitting astride his tummy and him telling me stories, you know, all these wonderful Indian stories. I trailed him all over! At Queen's he took up mining and engineering. Then he was sent up north to Sudbury, to the nickel mines there, and he had an accident, the machinery broke and a belt flew or something and hit him, and pulled his hand into some gears and his hand was crushed. He was told he'd never have complete use of his hand, his fingers were so crushed. So when he recuperated he came back to the farm. My mother's sister was a nurse, and they lived right across the road, so she was able to come over and dress his hand. He recovered and went back and got his degree and he got his job in Ottawa, in the Department of Mines, and that's where he served. He married a girl from Kingston.

My father's home was like his home when he came and we had such good visits. I was in high school then and telling him some of my problems, and he said, "Just remember, they won't accept you until you prove that you're better than they are. If your marks are good and if you conduct yourself properly and with dignity, then you'll make it." His motto was, "You'll make mistakes, but those that matter won't mind, and those that mind won't matter at all." He was my role model. When I had hard times in school, I would just remember what he told me.

When I finished high school, he and his wife invited me to come to Ottawa for six weeks. At that time there was the British Commonwealth and they had a this big conference in Ottawa that year. There were all kinds of parties and balls. I got the biggest charge out of helping them get ready for two big dos at Rideau Hall. He was so handsome in his full dress, you know white tie and tails. I helped put the studs in his shirt. And my aunt in her beautiful satin gown. Real satin. I helped her on with her long white gloves. Oh, it was exciting for this little eighteen-year-old girl. I did get to go to the garden party at Rideau Hall. The Prime Minister was R.B. Bennett. I was worried that I didn't have anything good enough to wear, but my Uncle helped me pick out something. I had been working picking berries for spending money, and I earned money for clothes. So I had this little dress that was pink and it was long with a peplum around the waist. It had puffed sleeves and a ruffle and tiny little flowers on the cloth. It was a nice dress. Oh, I thought I was grand, with my pretty pink dress and white gloves. My aunt wore a blue lace dress and a big picture hat. Uncle said we both looked great. The garden party, all the people from Africa in their traditional dress, the women from India in their beautiful saris, their beautiful silk. The men with their turbans. We were served champagne cocktails in little glasses. People brought them around to all the guests. Fancy sandwiches and fancy cakes. I was so excited, I couldn't eat anything. I remember the Prime Minister taking a lot cakes off the tray and pop them into his mouth like peanuts! It was such a happy time. I enjoyed every minute of it. My Uncle took me to his office and to the museum, they took me to all the places. I enjoyed most listening to the Carillon bells in the Parliament building. What a lucky girl I was!

Then I went to teacher's college, Normal School they called it in those days. And it was in Hamilton. So I boarded at the Y and walked, oh about a mile and a half, I guess, every morning and noon. I could go home on the bus on weekends, but often, during the winter, I stayed. I had a roomate at the Y, another girl from back north, and she and I became very good friends. In fact, we still visit back and forth. And there was another Native person who was also there at teacher's college. I really enjoyed that year in Hamilton, There wasn't the kind of discrimination like I had in high school.

I came back to the reserve and that was when they were trying to get Native teachers, they were giving Native teachers preference over the whites. So I was placed at School Number 6, among the Cayuga people, so I was teaching the children of my old playmates. They were such wonderful people, and I think there were only eight in my class who weren't traditional. One family went to the United Church, some others went to the Anglican. All the others were Longhouse People. My janitor was one of the Speakers in the Longhouse. And I always told him, I said, "I would never have gotten through my first year of teaching if it hadn't been for you." He was the janitor and I had some big boys in the school and he said, "If those boys ever give you any trouble, you just go and ring that bell and I'll be over here, and I'll fix them." Anyway, he gave me lots of support and I had great respect for that man. He's gone on now, and so is his son that I started in school. I was talking to his grandson this summer, about our people. Oh, he was a great man.

I attended funerals and other feasts in the Longhouse. I can understand Cayuga, but not speak it too well. And my mother never taught me Mohawk, you know, even though she and Dad spoke the language. But they were given the strap if they spoke it in school. I guess they thought they had to obey the government's wishes, and so I wasn't allowed to learn my own language.

My mother taught me the value of good work. I was an only child, so I had a lot of household duties. And I helped milk cows, and gathered eggs, fed chickens, went after the cows when they were out in the pasture. I had a dog that was called Dog, all I had to do was open the door and he would come for me. Oh, I had a happy, happy childhood! I was never lonely, I had playmates and relatives, and our house was sort of a gathering place for the family. Sometimes, there were so many people in our house, I never knew how Mother managed everything. One time, there were fourteen of us in the house. People stayed overnight and they told ghost stories. I was never afraid of the stories. There were supposed to be ghosts in the woods, but we weren't afraid. Thinking back, I just had a wonderful life. No regrets at all.

Family ties aren't what they used to be. I think they were stronger among Native people. I suppose I lived a sheltered life. It seemed that if there was anything frightening or scary, or if anything happened in the community that was not "for children's ears," the conversation would stop when the children entered the room. We never heard any of the scummier things in life, you know. A lot of things, I was completely unaware of. I used to walk five miles on the highway, and I would take rides. An old car would stop and I'd get in and tell him where I wanted to get off. We just trusted everyone, and you know, you trusted your own people. Now it's an altogether different world. I don't know, I really worry about my grandchildren. I'm very concerned for their future. It's so hard on young people. Especially Native youngsters. If you can't trust your own people, how can we ever survive? But I had the best of family love and support. I am very thankful.

Marjorie Hill, 1914 –

My mother was Catherine Claus, but she died and her sister took me and raised me. It wasn't until I was seven that I knew my aunt wasn't my mother. But I carried on with their name, Smith, until I had to be legal! Then I used my own name which was Duncan. Levi Brant's grandson was my first husband, and I had eight children by him. And there's only four of them living. I grew up on the Reserve, just a few houses east of the Seniors' building up there. I used to walk to school there, and then walked to the high school in Deseronto. I finished all but one year, then I fell in love. What fools we were!

I had a happy childhood. I was so much loved. When my father married a second time, he went to the States and took my brothers to live with him. So, it wasn't like I ever missed him or loved him. He didn't miss me, did he?! But my aunt was my mother and she gave me all the love a child could have. They didn't have any children of their own, so I was the apple of their eye. I had lots of kids to play with, the neighborhood kids and Aunt Maggie and Uncle Herb had all those kids and they were my playmates. I liked school, I should have gone further in school. Of course, you learn these things too late. I think I had the ability to do a lot more than I did, but it wasn't important at the time.

Yes, it was fun growing up. It took a very small excuse to get up

Marjorie Hill and parents, Fred and Lydia

a house party. Which is what most people did for fun in those days. Make us a cake, make some sandwiches, and off you'd go to someone's house. Somebody would play the fiddle, Uncle Tom for one, and I would play the piano, and we'd have a dance. Square dance, step-dancing. It was great fun. And when I was going to school, we used to dance at recess in the basement. Somebody'd play a mouth organ, and off we'd go! There wasn't really any discrimination in my case, but I was half Mohawk, and my skin wasn't as dark. But I know the others had a rough time. That's the way it was. It might still be that way. In fact, I'm sure it's still that way. Indians are the ones that are looked down on.

I always sort of knew my first husband. He was a Brant. I lived on Reserve until I inherited this house. And at that time my marriage was falling all apart. My first husband was, well, I don't know whether you could say he was an alcoholic, but he drank a lot. So when I was given this house, I very quickly moved into it with all my kids. And all I had to do was bring myself and my kids, it was fully furnished. I was so lucky. You see, the woman who gave me the house was my mother's first cousin, and I guess she knew what my life was like, and maybe she thought that one day I would need a place to call my own, so she gave me this place. Oh, I was lucky all right. I worked all through the marriage when I wasn't having a trail of babies. I did housework, and when my youngest boy was thirteen I got this job in Belleville, cleaning a newspaper's offices. Then I answered this ad and went to work for a family in Belleville. They had three children and they were just wonderful, one of the better things that's happened to me in my life. Even after I stopped working for them, I still get a cheque from them at Christmas. I did all the housework, and they had a ten room house with four bathrooms! I did everything, even the shopping, the cooking. Went up every morning, came home at night and do the same thing at home. Oh, sometimes I would be so tired.

My maternal grandparents lived at where Purple Acres is now. I remember them well and they spoiled me I guess because my mother had died. She was only twenty-eight and died of pneumonia, which is such a simple thing now. It's like my children that passed away. One little girl died from nephritis which is curable today. And one died with a leaking valve, which is curable today, she only lived six weeks. And one was struck by a truck when she was six and a half, and well, I guess she had a fractured skull, but she never lost a drop of blood and I think that was the problem. It was all inside. Then I lost my boy when he was fifty. So much of my life with my first husband is like a blur. So much sadness and hectic times, working and trying to feed my family. Some memories are not so good. But I moved here and couldn't get a divorce, it just wasn't possible, money-wise. But when Legal Aid came in I got a divorce and then I married my second husband. We were married in Christ Church. Kay and Lennox stood up for us. Oh, we had fun at that wedding. They went with us on our honeymoon. We went to Tweed where my husband's sister lived, so we didn't go far. But we had a great weekend!

I never had a silver spoon in my life and never expected one. I never expected much. If you could live in reasonable decency and respectability, why, that's all that was required. You make your own way. But I think, the way the Reserve is going now, they don't encourage people to make their own way. And maybe kids don't know how to do hard work. What will happen when the government doesn't give out any more money to Indians? I believe in higher education, but I believe in hard work too. Oh, I wouldn't want anyone to be poor like we were, but I worry that when there's no more money, what are the people going to do? We didn't have any money, but we grew our food and we exchanged work for food and all that. It didn't cost money to grow gardens, but hardly anybody gardens anymore. I use my composter and I have a little pail in the kitchen where I keep my scraps. I don't empty it, only when it gets full, saves myself steps, you know. Use my head and save my feet! My feet don't work too good.

Everybody spoke Mohawk then. But they'd stop talking it when the children came around. Because the schools taught that speaking Mohawk was not the thing to do. So the old folks clammed up and tried to only speak English with the children. There's been many changes around here since I was a girl. C31 changed a lot of things.

It's funny that all of a sudden the government was saying that women were Indians again! So stupid. I never had status until I got married, even though I was more Indian than these white women who married Indian men. But that was because my mother married a non-Indian. Anyway, they couldn't take away my living on Reserve. I always had that and a happy childhood.

I know there's talk of a Longhouse being built on Reserve. I don't know what to think of it. I've always been Anglican, and I remember when people used to come to church. People came in horse and buggies and lumber wagons. And people used to walk to church. We all got together on Sundays and sang and prayed. I wonder if there's a Longhouse, if people will come the way they used to come to church. Or will they find excuses like they do now. When I was a child, I just always thought that Mohawks were Anglicans! Now I know different, but I still wonder if people haven't got time for the religious side of life anymore. It's too much bother for some of them. But there's a need for some kind of moral uplift. Men fathering children, then leaving their families. That's not right. And the drinking and not working. I miss the way we used to all be a family. You knew everybody and probably were related to most of the people! It's not like that now. Why, some people don't even know their family history.

I have always quilted since I was ten. Always quilted. It was just something that you picked up from watching the women. No one really taught it to me. And I used to lye my own corn from scratch. You had to have hardwood ashes. And we'd sift them and make them a nice, fine powder, you know. And we had an old iron pot that would sit right in the hole in your stove, where you put the wood. You put your ashes in the pot and cover them with water and let it come to a boil and stir it a couple of times. Let it come to a good boil and set it outside on the ground. And it would all settle. And you'd pour the water off the top and that was your lye and it was so strong, you'd have to dilute it to make your corn.[1] And that's how I learned it. Years later, you could buy the lye and it was so much easier. But just recently I thought to myself, I'd like to make it once more with hardwood ashes, but nobody was burning wood. Couldn't get any hardwood ashes. And I was up at Ike Hill's one day and I said that to him. He says, I've got some ashes I'll give you. So he went in a little side room and brought out a brown bag full of ashes. So I brought them home and thought, well, I guess I'll lye some corn with these ashes. So I opened the bag and they were full of egg shells

Marjorie Hill with grandmother and mother

and bottle caps and cigarette butts! Well, I cleaned it up and made my lye and did the corn. I just wanted to do that once more, like the old days. We always canned and preserved our food. It was a lot of work, especially for the women, but we had to do it if we wanted to feed our families. We had to do a lot of things that took hard work. But I don't regret any of it. Still, I'm thankful for lye that I can buy at the store!

1. Lyed corn is also known as hominy.

Mel Hill, 1918 – 1993

In them days it was altogether different. I remember my father getting up in the morning, the first thing he'd do is look around at all the houses, make sure there was smoke coming out of them. If no smoke, he'd go and see what was the matter with them. Today, you could be dead before anyone would say something. It's an awful difference. Money, money, everybody's after money, that's the big thing, that's what I see. Nobody got paid for anything in them days, they never had any money, but they had a lot of fun. We used to pick dandelions, you know, my aunt over here made dandelion wine. And for a berry box full she'd give us five cents. Well, hell, it would take you all day because she'd make sure you didn't put no stems or nothing, just the blossoms. She'd go right through them before she paid a nickel.

Nobody was afraid of work like they are today, seems to me. They want their own jobs, they want to get an education and say how much money they're going to get, what job they want and everything else. Education's a good thing to a point, but I can't see everybody going through for degrees when there's no jobs in the degree area. Why don't they go through for electrician and plumbers and where the jobs are? They can't get the kids to take up them trades, builders and stuff like that. But nobody wants to do the manual work, everybody wants to be the boss! That's the problem, that's what I see. They get their M.Ed or B.A. and then they're walking down the street not working. And I think welfare's the worst thing that ever happened here. Just to sit home and get in a rut, that's what they're in now. Seems like everybody's unemployed here and living on welfare. It makes you feel bad about yourself, welfare.

I was born in this house. I've been here ever since. Only time I was away was during the war, and I was in Buffalo for four years before I come home and went to Canadian army. I went with the engineers, through Kingston, and landed on D-Day in France. Nobody could have told us we were going to die. We figured we lost one-third of the boys the first day we landed. Terrible, terrible how people can get killed. As close as you were and you're still alive. There musta been six or seven of us Native men in a field company of 265 men. We're having a reunion next month. I don't know how many of the men got killed, but it was the darn reinforcements that got killed because there weren't enough training. We used to get mad because we had to train over and over again. You got into action, you didn't have time to think, you reacted right away. So my training paid off. It saved our lives. I was twenty-one, but there was a lot of them only sixteen or seventeen.

One of my friends, he's my best friend yet, he was only sixteen and we were in Terrace, B.C. and he got scarlet fever, and he had a temperature of 104. They tied him on one of those stretchers, you know that they carry, what the army has, strapped him on because he was delirious and they had to put him in a straight-jacket, shoved him in a box car and sent him up to Prince Rupert, ninety miles away. I was at the train when they pushed him on and I thought I lost him. Wasn't three weeks later and I got scarlet fever and I went up and I was right in the next bed to him. And he still tells me, he says, "Mel, if it wasn't for you, I would have died because I had given up." After I got in up there, we got to talking and I got him interested in Indians. He knows more about Indians now than I do, because he studied while I worked. He even tells me about Joseph Brant and all the kids and everything! Yes, siree.

We get together about three times a year for our reunion. Boy, they look after me good. I have to get up and take pills in the morning and I have to have something to eat because of my sugar. They never eat breakfast until 11 o'clock, they get up and go. But they get up and make toast for me, they look after me real good. And at night, if I got up in the night, I wouldn't hit the floor and they'd be up, "Mel, you okay?" Oh yeah, they look after me, they're good friends. All my friends, you know they're something else. Always said they were closer than brothers, because you lived with them for four years, through life and death, you know. They'd do anything for you and you'd do anything for them. Sometimes even brothers are not that close. But that war was tame to what's going on over there in that Sarajevo. Them people haven't got nothing to defend themselves. Oh dear, terrible. And those poor people in Germany, those Turkish people, getting killed by those Germans. This is a terrible world.

When I was a kid, you'd start working at about five or six years old. Once you were able to go a little bit, you had nothing but your work to do. If you didn't get your work done you never got no supper, you went to bed without it. Mom and Dad were strict in a lot of ways, but they were good parents just the same. My dad lived until ninety-three and I had an uncle lived till ninety-nine. He lived in Florida and we were down there just a week before he died. He was ninety-nine and he spent one day in the hospital. He was standing up and shook hands with us, and we had pictures taken on the day we left on the 5th of January, and he died on the 12th. That's his carvings up there, that owl up behind you and different things he carved. He was always carving. He worked about two hours a day right up until he died. He had a little shack, one of those tin shacks they have now, all his carving tools and his carvings and he'd go there and do two hours a day. He says, "I'm going to have shrimp for supper tonight." I said, "Well, let me go and get the shrimp. "No, he says, "I'm going to go and catch them and I'm gonna fix them." And he did. He died on the 12th. I guess he was what you'd call an artist. He kicked himself that he never come back here. He lived to be ninety-nine because he always worked hard and never drank.

My mother and father spoke the language, but you see, they took the language away from us when I got to school. They would punish us at the Mission School. There's a few of the old-timers still got the language, but I was punished. We all were! Darn government taking away the language. I had some good teachers. There was a white woman who got to be very interested in Indians. She stayed here seven years and used to come back here to visit. She wrote a thesis on Molly Brant. There's a few books on Molly, then the government put the postage stamp out of her, and there was quite a to-do when they put the stamp out. We were down there when they put the stamp out, took a bunch down there, us Indians. Seemed like there should be Indians down there, us Mohawks and Molly.

I went up to third year in high school which was pretty good. Then in '37 I went to Buffalo. I ran away from home, you see. I ran away from home when I had two or three older brothers and they was all at home. I was the youngest and I had to do what my dad told me. The others were all twenty-one or older so they could do what they liked. That's the way the Indian family was run. Once you got of age, you could pretty near do what you wanted to do. We had a car, and the older boys would take the car on Saturday night and go away. I'd have to do the chores, finish them up, and I got fed up. So I run away, ran all the way to Buffalo.

I had bought a calf for 65 cents when it was just born, and I raised it to two years old and I sold it to the butcher in town. He come up and gave me $35 for it. That's how much money I had when I left. I struck out to go to the tobacco country where I was going to make big money, working with tobacco. Well, I was just two weeks too early, and there was two or three of them wanted to give me a job on their farms and I says, "I just left the farm, I don't want to do more farming, I want to get where I can make some money." Well, I got on the highway and I would be thumbing west and there would be no car coming. But I could have ended up in Detroit just as easy. A guy come, a young fella come along with a brand new car, he just come to Detroit to pick it up, and he picked me up and says, "Where you going?" And I says, "Where you going?" He says, "I'm going to Buffalo." And I says, "I guess I'll go to Buffalo." And he said, "How are you going to get across the border?" So, I showed him my Indian card. Well, he didn't know much about Indian cards, but when he got to the border he says, "I've got an Indian fella with me." They never asked me a question, just "Okay, go on."

It wasn't like it was way back in 1903. My mother told me that the exhibition was on in Buffalo, and every one of our generation there was a red-head, 'cause they mixed up with the Dutch down there, down in the Mohawk Valley back then. So, this one Uncle of mine had red, red hair, and they was on the train, and the white people come along and asked them questions, and the family says they were all Indians. I guess the conductor started asking Uncle a lot of questions and *he* started talking Mohawk and telling the conductor how stupid he was and everything else, and they all got laughing. He said the awfullest things about that young conductor in Indian, they was just making a big joke out of the conductor, so he let them in. That's a time the language come in handy. Another one of my uncles up here, he made a little moonshine, so the Mounties come to raid him. So they was questioning him and questioning him, and he says to his son in Mohawk, "Go down and pull the plug on that barrel downstairs." The son went down and pulled the plug; by the time they got done talking there was no evidence, it was down the drain. That was my father's brother. Oh, there's a lot of funny things going on down here. But the language come in handy sometimes, especially when there's white folks around.

I had an aunt and uncle in Buffalo, so when I got there I went to the hotel where my uncle worked. I went in and he says, "Where did you come from Mel?" I says, "I just come from home." So he says, "Have you seen Aunt Elsie?" I says, "No, I don't even know where you live!" He gave me ten cents and told me what streetcar to get on, and called Aunt to meet me at the station. I got on that thing and the guy told me when to get off and she was down there waiting. And I stayed with them for two weeks, then I got a job as a stevedore on the boats. Oh, they took care of me. You never worried about food if you had relatives around. That's the Indian way.

When I got in the Army, I ended up being the cook. I was a corporal and in charge of twelve men. I had a guy come to me, and I was supposed to designate someone for cook, but they wouldn't go for it, they said, "You're the cook, Mel." Half the time we was over there I was cooking. And you know in Belgium and Holland, they don't eat corn on the cob. Think it's feed for the farm animals. So I says to the boys, "If you see any corn fields, you get some corns." They brought them back and I cooked it; threw a cup of sugar in it. Even if it was field corn, it was better than nothing.

The first Christmas we had in England, my mother sent me dried corn, beans and parsnips. So, I says to the guy in charge, "Any chance of getting some pork bones, and I'll make us some soup." Well, you know you got to soak the beans overnight, and you've got to soak the corn overnight. Next day I went in the kitchen and they says to me, "What the hell kind of soup you making if it takes two days to make a pot of soup?" I says, "Don't worry about it." So I brought all the Indian boys in for breakfast of corn soup. Every country I was in, that's the first thing we did, make corn soup. I had a little white fella from Saskatchewan, and he says, "Keep feeding me that soup. I could live on that soup. I says, "Well, some of us do live on that soup!" I always had corn in my bag. Maybe it protected me from getting killed like so many of those boys.

I had a little trouble in the army when I first come in because I was Native. I just rode it out. I just said to myself, if they're gonna discriminate against me from the start, what the heck am I going to do? A lot of Indians just went home and sent their uniforms back, 'cause they couldn't conscript them. I went in for basic training in Peterborough, and about a month in, there was a hockey game with a Peterborough team and one from Belleville. And it said on our orders if anybody went to the hockey game, they could have an all-night pass. Well, we didn't want to see the hockey game, but we wanted to come home. There was guys from Belleville and one from Kingston, and they says we'd go and get our tickets and go home for the night and come back the next day. I was the one that got out of the bus and bought the five tickets. And I went through the door and the lady tore them in two. I never noticed, but when we had to turn in the stubs the next day, there was only four ticket stubs. So, I was the one they pegged for being AWOL, and I was the only Indian. And that just burned me up! They put me up on charges and I said "Not guilty." They said, what do you got? Well, I said, bring that bus driver down here, he'll remember me. And the bus driver says, "Yeah, I remember that Indian." So they had to throw out the charges. But it got to me that they was going to be watching my every move and I thought, it's bad enough I gotta fight a war, but I gotta fight these guys too? Yes, I had some trouble, but I let it roll off of me. And some of those guys that give me trouble never made it back, and that's a darn shame. Horrible thing, war.

When we landed on D-Day, we had two battleships, the Nelson and the Rodney and they were throwing fire out as big as this table. The Germans were fighting like hell, they just come out of the holes like rats. They had tunnels right through the whole city. If they got cornered, they just went in the hole and came out the other end. Terrible, isn't it? There was a lot of mistakes made, you know. The worst of it is, the darn officers, they sit back behind the lines and made the decisions about what we were going to do, and half the time they was wrong. I seen all those bodies lying around and I like to get sick, thinking about them officers sitting around, giving orders. All those boys. Me and Verna went back there in '88, and it's like nothing ever happened there, except for the cemetary and some of the French people who still remember the Canadians. I never could feel comfortable about the Germans after that. Oh, I know that's wrong to be that way, but they just did so many awful things, especially to the Jewish people. Imagine what they would have done to the Indians if they got a chance. Yeah, but we had plenty done to us right here. I guess the Germans weren't the only ones trying to get rid of people that had a right to live. You know, this was our land, all of it. And we took such good care of it too. Oh dear, it was all so bad.

When I came back from the war, I says to my brothers, "I'll do the work from now on, and I'll be the boss." They said okay and gave me the farm. I wasn't as easy-going as my father. We had a cousin up the road and if he went by when we was killing pigs, he'd always stop and ask to borrow a ham. He'd say, "When I kill mine, I'll bring it back to you." He never even had a pig! But my dad would let him have it. So when I took over, he come by and tried the same game, but I told him I worked on the cash and carry basis. He must have been real sorry my dad wasn't around no more! But the kids today, they just want to borrow and borrow and get themselves so far in debt, they're crying bankrupt at age twenty-five! We never borrowed money. 'Course, they wouldn't have lent us any anyways. Indians couldn't borrow money then. Now the kids have credit cards and such. It worries me that we got into bad habits from the white folks.

During the Depression we just kept from one day to the next. There was no hunger, but there was no money either. But them days, you never took, you worked hard for whatever. We never suffered, we went through the whole thing, and had enough to eat. You could always feed people coming in. Two or three days they stayed, some of them a week. But we had lots of potatoes, and sometimes a barrel of pork, lots of everything. We'd play cards and go to the neighbors and play some more cards and go on hayrides and stuff like that. I think we had more fun then than we ever have now. We were still in the horse and buggy days. In the winter we had sleighs and we used to get a sleighload every Friday night and go down to the east end of the reserve. The next Friday they'd come up here to dance, we'd dance all night. Fiddles, step-dancing, oh, we had fun. See that beam above me where the light is? Well, we'd dance till midnight and Dad would put up a big hook and hang a trapeze and we'd do all sorts of tricks, then go back to the dancing. Oh yeah, this is a solid house, it was moved here in 1883 when the well went dry in the other place. My grandfather moved the house over here. He was tough, but so was my dad. He worked and worked on this farm, then he'd go and help somebody else. The neighbors always helped each other. Today, your neighbors hardly know each other. How could that be?

Verna and I were engaged in 1945, and then we broke up and she married someone else and had five kids, then we got married fifteen years ago. She was teaching school and didn't want to live on a farm.

And I said, well I'm going to farm, so there's no use in us carrying on because we both can't get our ways. So we lived apart all those years, but we got together again and got married. She had an alcoholic husband. Alcohol has been a curse to Indians. It hasn't been too bad here, but we got it just the same. There's a few that have ruined their lives. But up North it's bad. I've travelled up there when I was Chief, and it's terrible bad. There was a guy up there, I don't think he weighed a hundred pounds and I just about cried. He said when he was younger, his father would go out hunting, and they'd stay in bed till he came back. And if he had something, they'd get up, or stay in bed till the next day, because maybe the next day he'd get something if he wasn't drinking. I just about cried. Pitiful. I was Chief here for seven years, and I heard all kinds of bad stories when I travelled and even some from here.

I think we're getting to the time when we're going to have to pay taxes. If we want self-government and all that, we've got to pay for something! I think we got to realize that if we want the government out of our lives, we got to pay. How else are we going to survive? Some of the larger reserves have natural resources, and they'll be able to take care of their people. But we don't have any left and I worry about our land being sold off to white people. We need to figure out what self-determination means to *us*. If it means doing our own thing until we run out of money, then begging the government for more, well forget it. We got too used to handouts from the government, first on welfare, then on grants and such. Maybe we got too much money, and then everybody started getting greedy like the whiteman. That's not the right way.

I hear that there's talk of putting up a Longhouse here. Well, you got to live right if you're Longhouse. No greedy stuff, or stealing, or drinking, or not taking care of your family, all of them. You got to know the language too. I hear that somewhere out there, Indian folks are giving Clans to white people! You can't get a Clan. You've got to get it from your mother and she's got to be Indian. When I was a kid nobody wanted to be Indian, now everybody wants to be one! We were the poorest people and the run-down people, and nobody wanted to even say they were, even the Indians themselves! But it's crazy, I don't know what's going on. Suddenly, everything's changed, and people want to be Indian. I wonder if they'd like to be poor, too. Not much chance of that, eh?

When we used to have Indian agents, they were the dictator. When I come back from overseas, we had a lot of veterans who had their money sent home, but we didn't know that the money was sent to the Indian agent who wasn't giving it to the families. So, we called a meeting and the agent came and said, "What's your business?" I says, "Yeah, I got some business and I say you've got too much damn say around here and you're stealing our money!" Oh, geez, he went up four feet in the air, grabbed his papers and ran down the road. But later, we got rid of him, and he cried like a baby when he had to go. When he left here, he had two houses in Deseronto, he had a brand new car, and he had two kids going to university. Now he didn't do that on the god-damn agent's pay! Everything was his. Terrible. I said, "We've been fighting them dictators all for years now, why should we put up with one here?" We've had some bad ones here. They'd get themselves named as executors of wills and steal everything. They'd come right in the house after somebody died and go through all the things to see if there was anything worth taking. I was glad when we got rid of them once and for all.

I was going to do a book, but I'm getting tired now. This whole house is filled with stuff, papers and books about our history. You know, if people want to find out anything about this reserve they say, "Go over to Mel's. If he don't know it, nobody does." And you know, I get all kinds of people coming over and asking me stuff, asking to see this or that. I like the visitors, but I'm getting a little tired now. And sometimes I like to go play Bingo and I'm not at home. Verna is always on the go. You know, our name didn't used to be Hill. Back then, we all had Indian names, Mohawk names. But the government couldn't keep track of us 'cause they couldn't pronounce the names, so they up and give us Christian names like Hill and so on. When Thunderwater was around here, he wanted people, Indian people to claim their Native rights. I guess one of them would've been our own names. I feel bad that I don't know what our Indian name is. I tried to trace it, but didn't have any luck. If somebody finds it, I'd like to see it. It would be something to see.

Helen Brant, 1920 –
& Cameron Brant, 1919 –

CAMERON: A lot of them young kids now, they don't know their relations. They don't have parents that sit down on the couch and tell them history, you know.

HELEN: Some kids don't even know their own clan! Why, my own sister-in-law phoned the other day and said, what was your mother's Clan? I said Wolf, and I said, your husband should have known that, 'cause you take your mother's Clan, not your father's. Our Clan is Wolf. My mother always used to tell us that. You got to tell the young kids that, or they'll never know.

CAMERON: I was born in my grandparents house. My mother died when I was two, so I just dream about her. My sister was nine months old when Mother died, my brother was four. He says he can remember her. He used to tell me stories about her. So, my grandparents took us and raised us. We made our own entertainment in those days. Skating on the creek, game of hockey, play ball if we could find a field to play in.

HELEN: My parents always farmed, ever since I can remember.

We lived over there on a hill. My father worked on the railroad, he started when he was nineteen. My mom and us kids were on the farm while he worked out. He was a good dad. He always worked out, gave Mom all the money so she could control the table. And then we had stuff on the farm; chickens, geese. We always had enough to eat. My parents were good parents. No carousing or forgetting they had children. Dad used to walk clear over to Marysville every morning. Then in the summer he'd live here. Kids wouldn't do that today.

CAMERON: That was a terrible job at that time. I worked on the railroad too. It was hard work. Then they gradually got machinery and stuff like that. Got layed off, didn't need men, they had machinery!

HELEN: We were seven when we started school. I cried if I couldn't go to school, I liked it that much! I had a white teacher, but there was a Native teacher....Frank Maracle?

CAMERON: I didn't finish grade eight.

HELEN: You didn't because you had to go and work! He had chores to do before he went to school and chores to do when he come back.

CAMERON: Like I say, I didn't get all of grade eight. But then I travelled around a little bit. This is a great experience, travelling. You get to meet different people. Then, when I worked on the railroad, I had a job that was just myself and one helper. Them helpers was going and coming. I was getting to meet all kinds of nationalities. They told me about their countries and all that stuff. I learned a lot from them. Then I was in the Army and I went overseas during the war.

HELEN: You weren't active. Because you got sick, German measles, they put you in the hospital.

CAMERON: I got the measles.

HELEN: German measles. They put him in the hospital and then he got better. Well, they were supposed to release him from the army before he even left here, because of his flat feet, eh.

CAMERON: I questioned that, you know. I didn't know why they sent me overseas. But I was held in England. They posted me to the General Hospital, so I worked down in the hospital with the patients. I used to get them books or whatever they'd need. If they were doing handicrafts, I'd help them. It was just temporary, but finally they made me a corporal before I left. But that was quite interesting, going to the different hospitals. I was the only Native in my regiment, but I got to meet other Natives. I can't say that we were treated too differently from the rest. But like I say, there was so many nationalities of all kinds. Lots of times I think about how we all worked together, all of us. Don't know why we can't do that any more.

HELEN: We spoke Mohawk in the family. I still speak it when I can find somebody to talk it.

CAMERON: We all spoke Mohawk. I don't understand why it stopped. I guess the government didn't like it. So much of what we did the government didn't like.

HELEN: Yes, but they're teaching the kids Mohawk at the school, and that's good.

CAMERON: Yeah. They should have been teaching it all along. So much of the old words could tell you about your people. Maybe if the kids are learning Mohawk, they'll learn about us.

HELEN: Everything has changed so much. TV, videos, all that stuff just interferes with children. They don't get to learn hard work, or sit down with the family and talk Mohawk. I know people got to work. I still work, sewing at the factory; but we used to be able to sit with the children and tell them things.

CAMERON: Yeah. It seems like nobody just sits with their kids and tells them stuff. My grandparents always told me stories, or found time to answer questions I might have. And some even neglect their own family!

HELEN: Yes. That's a sad thing. It's not the way it used to be. But times change. I just wish it wouldn't change so much for us here. I'm glad people aren't so poor like we used to be. But, we didn't know we were poor. We had plenty to eat. And my parents saw that we did. They didn't think the government should do what the parents were supposed to do. We had to work hard, what's wrong with that?

CAMERON: Nothing. You did what you had to do. But it wasn't a bad life. Like I said, I met a lot of interesting people in my day. You can't get that by watching the television. And you can't learn hard work or how to raise kids by watching the tv. We're getting old, eh?!

Helena Pfefferle, 1921 –

Before I was born, my dad worked at the mill. He broke his leg, it wasn't set right, and well, he was lame after that. After the mill shut down, why there was no work. If you didn't have a farm, you were in trouble. My mother worked, too. She would go out and help people. Sometimes she'd get paid a bit of money. I would have had lots of brothers and sisters if they had lived, but so many died. I ended up with two brothers and one sister. I was born at home, of course. We had midwives then, or sometimes a doctor would come to the house. But that costs money.

I went to school, but in the summertime we went out picking, or husking corn. They used to provide places to live, like a boarding house. Families were allotted a place to live. All you needed was a place to sleep. Everybody worked, even the little kids. Picking berries, tomatoes, husking corn. When one place was finished, we'd go to the next. It was like that all summer long. So, I went to school up until Senior Second, but I had to stop when my mom got sick. I knew she was sick for a long time, she had a lot of ailments. But I had to stop school and take on work at home.

When my mother started school, she couldn't speak a word of English. At that time, they wouldn't let you speak Mohawk. And when the people saw how it was, they just stopped teaching their children Mohawk. What was the use, if you were just going to be punished for it? I would dearly love to speak the language of my mother, but I'm too old to learn now, eh?

My first *real* job was when I was fourteen or fifteen. Working in a factory. I worked in factories all my life, or the cannery. When I was pregnant, I still went out tomato picking! It was mostly Natives doing the picking. They'd send big trucks over here, and took the people to work the fields. Maybe I got paid 10 or 15 cents an hour. I went up finally to 50 cents an hour. It sounded pretty good back then. Times was bad then.

Things have changed. People are different. If people needed to raise a barn or fix the roof, you'd go help. Now, people want top dollar just for helping their neighbors. No wonder everybody is surprised that the sense of family is disappearing. You used to do things because we were all one family here at Tyendinaga. That's changed. And I think that's a very poor way to get along. And too many folks are marrying non-Indians. There never used to be many non-Natives living here. Now, we've got them all over the place, telling us what to do. I think that's what the government wants. Indians to marry non-Indians, then pretty soon there won't be no

Helena Pfefferle

Indian blood left and they can come in and take our land. Education is good, up to a point, but if it makes you unsatisfied with who you are, then I say it's not good for us.

My first husband I knew when I was a kid. I knew him for a long time when we got married. He died when he was just going on to his thirtieth year. I lost my status when I married my last husband. I wasn't too happy about that. It was unfair. The men around here could marry whoever they wanted and *they* didn't lose status. And the white women became Indians if they married a man from here! That's not right. I was happy when I got my status back, but I figured that I was always Mohawk, so a band card didn't mean a thing to me. But they acted as if I should be grateful for something I was all along!

My dad was very stern and strict. He wasn't mean or abused us, but he was just, too. He always listened to our side of the argument. Mom was a good mom. Oh, how she worked! She was a tiny person, but could work with the men and do her share and then some. I was lucky to have my parents. I mostly raised my children alone. And it was hard, but I did it. I have three grandchildren and seven great-grandchildren.

Well, you know, what you don't ever have, you never miss. So, I think I had a pretty good life. But the young ones don't know what we been through. They don't know that the old folks were punished if they spoke Mohawk, because now, they learn it in school. They don't know how hard it was to get something to eat or wear. I think this book is a good thing. If the young kids read it, they'll know that everything wasn't a bed of roses for the people here. Maybe education is teaching kids to be more like the whiteman. We had to learn things like how to get along in the world, how to garden, how to sew, how to take care of the family. I don't like to see Native people who are greedy, who think the government is going to supply everything they need. That's not the Indian way, the Mohawk way.

I lost all my family in a short space of time. First my mom, then dad, then my brother and sister. But I'm still here. We lost men during the War. Some was even at Dieppe. But the men that came back wouldn't talk about it. The women tried to help by knitting socks and stuff like that. We were all so poor though.

When we'd get sick, we couldn't call a doctor like you can now. So we knew which plants to use for fevers and such. I wish I could remember their names. Mom would go and collect them and put them in jars. Dad trapped muskrat. And in the spring we'd fish for pickerel. I liked the muskrat meat. Dad would sell the fur to some people in Belleville and Napanee. There were a lot of traplines here. I guess young people don't know how to trap anymore. Maybe they don't have the patience for it. They're used to going to a store and buying meat. We never even imagined that you could buy meat in a store all packaged up. It's a shame that more don't know about the medicines and the hunting and trapping. How did this happen?

I am troubled about the future. Children who don't respect their elders. People getting greedy and saying nasty things about their neighbors. Counting too much on the government for everything. There's talk of putting up a Longhouse here, but I don't know if it'll do any good. You got to use the Longhouse properly, and I don't know if the people are willing to give up the government laws or the Christian laws. It would be good if there was more of the old ways and old laws. We've come so far away from all that.

I remember the first movie I ever saw. "The Wizard of Oz." We went to Picton and it cost 10 cents to see it. I thought it was so great. I could have stayed there for a week! But I rarely got to do anything like that. It must have been a special holiday. I didn't have too many chances to play. We were always working or had chores. But I'll remember that movie forever. When my kids were little, there wasn't money to do special things or have treats. I'm sad about that. Oh yes, I think there was something with Shirley Temple in it that I saw too. Such pretty clothes; singing and dancing. She looked like a happy child.

We had a garden. And a patch of strawberries, great big strawberries. Watermelon, muskmelons, corn, cucumbers. There was a terrible storm and the hail just killed them all. Oh dear. My mother cried. We didn't have much and just to see it all gone. Oh dear. I learned to cook from my mom, but nowadays I don't cook except to make corn soup once in a while. It's no fun to cook for just one person. I'm not lazy, but cooking doesn't interest me anymore. Sometimes I don't remember how to cook! But the corn soup, *that* I remember how to make!

Ada Doreen, 1926 –

I was born Ada Maracle. I think five of my brothers and

sisters passed away before I was born. You know, they had no

medication like there is now, and besides, nobody cared if

Indian kids were sick.

My dad's father died when he was a boy and Dad was sent to Brantford to live because Grandma couldn't take care of the children. He was eighteen before he came home, and he never felt comfortable here because this wasn't home to him. But he stayed and married my mom and built the small house on the land where I was born.

My mother had eleven children. Five died and there was six of us to raise. Dad worked wherever he could and mom stayed home with us, but she worked! I only have a brother and sister left. My sister's in a nursing home and I miss her so much. I go see her but it's not the same as if she was here. We need to have a nursing home on the reserve. Our people don't want to leave and be taken care of by strangers. Our old people want to be with their relatives, their own kind. My mom brought our grandfather to live with us when he took sick. Our house had one room, and that was our living room, our bedroom, our den, our everything! So we had this one room and put Grandpa's bed there, and I remember standing fanning him, oh day in and day out. He had cancer and had a tube in his jugular, and he was bringing up blood. Well, I had to hold the basin while Mom had to reach into his throat and bring out these big clots of blood, eh. And I held the basin and was plastered in blood.

The week before he died, he took each of us kids and told us all something. If he'd been rushed off reserve and taken to a nursing home, I'd never have this to think about. He felt my arms and said, "Why, you poor slim thing, you're going to have a great big family." Well, how did he know that? But I ended up having ten children. He just knew. And my sister, well, he said, "You poor little thing, you're going to cause your mother a lot of grief, but it won't be your fault." Well, my sister married at seventeen and married a guy that wasn't awfully good to her, so she run away from

Ruth Maracle, Ada Maracle (Ada Doreen),
Bertha Maracle, Marion Brant, Audrey Brant

him and come to me. My mom was sick about it all. I was living in Hamilton and my sister would hitch-hike to me. She started having seizures, epileptic seizures. Many years later she went into a coma, then passed away. Oh, it was so sad, and I wonder if that guy she married had anything to do with it.

My mother and dad always talked Mohawk. But I never talked it, we weren't supposed to, you know. But I learned to understand what they were talking about. I'd watch them very close. I was a curious child. The older folks said not to speak it because they used to get a beating in school if they spoke it. When I got married and moved away, my husband and I would speak it to each other, just the odd phrase here and there. When my husband passed away and I moved back here, I had the opportunity to pick up on Mohawk through Jan Hill, bless her heart. She made all the arrangements for me to go to London (Ontario). Well, mind you, in London I didn't learn the Mohawk language, you had to know a certain percent of it, so they gave me a tape and a book. There were pictures in the book and we had to tell a story about the pictures. It took me three weeks to do this tape! My head would just be full of words! I did master it. I made my tape and sent it to London, then I was accepted at the College. So from then on, it just started growing and growing. I used to go to bed at night, just tossing and turning on the bed with all these things all going through my head. And I'd dream of my mom and dad, speaking in Mohawk, and it started to come alive again. I searched through all the dreams and memories, Lord, how I searched! It began bubbling out of me, unrolling. What a wonderful thing!

Some people might say what use is it to know Mohawk now? But I say we got to learn it and relearn it so we will always have it and it will never be taken from us again. The government took so much away from us, but if we got our language, there's a part of us they can't steal away. The language will be ours forever. So, I teach it now, but I wish I was twenty years younger. I get tired sometimes! So, I'm always pushing the language and telling the people don't be scared if you make mistakes. If you don't make mistakes, you'll never learn. And learning the language is the best thing we can do for our people.

When we were young, we never were told about the facts of life. We didn't know where babies came from. My mother told me she found me in the wood pile. I used to hurt so much about that. I felt I didn't really belong. And when I got pregnant with my first child, I didn't know what was the matter with me. I was sixteen years old, and didn't know a thing. My grandson, who is three, knows where babies come from. He sat there and told me! But, in my day, we were pretty ignorant about things like that. It wasn't easy being married that young. Mom helped a lot with my family. It was wartime and Amos went away. He didn't go out of the country though. But we were separated for four years, and I lived with my mom and dad, still living in that one room. I was awful lonely, being just a girl and married. So much I didn't know.

Both mom and dad died of cancer. I took care of them. Wouldn't consider any nursing homes or such things like that. The night she died she got up and danced across the floor, then I put her to bed. She said, "I'm ready now, I'm ready." So I kissed her goodnight and I walked out. My baby daughter, who was eight or nine, shared the same room. In the night, my daughter calls that grandma needs me. I jumped out of bed. My mother had fell. I hollered for my son, who came and picked his grandma up and held her hand until she passed away. It was nice that my son will always have that, that he was there and touching her when she went. These people that don't look after their families, they don't have that good feeling.

I liked school when I was young, but at first I ran away a lot. Scared, I guess. The truant officer would come to the house and bawl my parents out for not sending me to school. But sometimes I didn't have anything to wear and our shoes were so wore out that I couldn't walk to school. And they wouldn't let me in with bare feet. And I used to get awful bad headaches. My head would pound and pound. A doctor used to come to the school and give us check-ups. He said I needed glasses, but my parents couldn't afford glases for me, eh. So I missed a lot of school.

There wasn't much work around here when I got married. My

husband only pumped gas. We ended up in Aldershot, where Amos got a job at Cook's Cement Plant. He had several other jobs, he worked the longest at the Fuller Brush factory. When my baby was two years old, I got a job at the school, doing the cleaning work. I was there for seven years. I never had too many sick days, but I had to have an operation, a hysterectomy. They didn't do it right, so I started to bleed real bad when I got home, and they did another operation to save my life. I guess they should have done it right the first time!

Of course, things have changed here. There was a time when I could walk right across the Reserve and never be afraid of anything. And we worked hard for what we have. The government never gave a darn about us, except to tell us what to do. Now, people think the government is a savior. Well, I don't. They're the ones told us our language wasn't any good. And they're the ones took away my status because I married Amos and he was from St. Regis. He was as Indian as me, but wasn't registered. Can you imagine that?! If it wasn't for the Native women going to court, I'd still be considered a "foreigner." And I got to say this, the government did rule in our favour. Of course, it didn't have anything to do with them, but they still took our side, the Native women, I mean. The band wouldn't have given us our status back, those men didn't want all these women claiming their rightful place. Seems to me that some of these men were too much like white men, not giving respect to women. And everytime something goes wrong, they blame the women. There's Native women all across Canada and we're strong and we'll stick up for our rights. There are Native women in politics, in organizations that fight for Native people. Where would we be without the women?

Phyllis Green, 1927 –

I went to school on Reserve, then went to Deseronto High
School, and then to Ontario College, then I got married! I had
a lot of encouragement for going to school. I worked for a
while at Newcast Canning Factory till I started having my
family. In 1959, I was approached to work as secretary to the
Band Council. I worked for a while in the Indian Agency in
Deseronto until they moved onto the Reserve, into the house
where the Food Bank is now. I think that was in 1972. Then in
'75 they moved to where we are now. Yes, there have been a
lot of changes on Reserve.

My mother spoke Mohawk, and my grandparents spoke it all the
time. But in those days you were chewed out for speaking it, so I
never learned it. It wasn't encouraged, even though the old folks
spoke it every chance they got. And now we have classes. I think it's
a good idea, but if there's no older people that can help them put it
into sentences and everything else…you have to have somebody
talking it all the time, I think, to learn it. And Mohawk has different
dialects. My mother belonged to the Indian Homemakers' Associa-
tion and she used to go to all these different reserves, and she said
you could pick the dialect up. My mother was real active in the
Homemakers'. Aunt Minnie Brant brought it in here. I think it was
to help the northern reserves, because I remember my mother

making flannel pyjamas and nightgowns for infants, and such things as that, and then they made quilts and shipped them off to some place. Oh yes, the women would go to other reserves and have their meetings. That was quite the thing.

When we were young we skated every chance we got. We were out on the Bay, 25 below zero, skating. In summer we played ball, there wasn't much else to do. Got older, we were allowed to go

Phyllis Green

dance at the Council House once in a while. Mostly, we worked! We had a farm. We had cows. Dad had horses, we never ever had a tractor until later years, so everything was done by horses. And in the summer we tried to get jobs picking strawberries, cherries in Greenfield. We sure had to do our share of work and help around the house. We wore a lot of hand-me-downs, but we always had food on our table, never starved. We had no electricity, was coal oil lamps and wood stove. In fact, my parents didn't have electricity until 1952, and running water. Now kids today are spoiled, I guess. Because all they have to do is ask and they seem to get what they want. When we try to tell them what we went through, they don't believe it. We always walked to school, we had to walk to school, home for lunch, back again. Now, buses come to your doorstep.

I remember the Indian Agents. They were supposed to work in partnership with the Council, but they ended up being kind of the boss. We were talking self-government in '59, which we still haven't got. We always had the two parties here, the Longhairs and the Shorthairs, now there's a third party. And it seems like, every year there's more fighting and bullying going on. It's sad because I worry that somebody is going to get hurt. And I don't know how we would tax everyone if we had self-government. Some people can barely get by on pensions and if they had to pay taxes they'd be in sad shape. Some people say that us Indians have it made because you know, we're not paying taxes, or not paying for our medicine, but I mean, compared to everything else that's been taken away, all the land, well, it's a small thing.

Well, I lived on the edge of town, we lived on the Bayshore Road. The houses were scattered, but they were within walking distance. My nearest neighbor was just below the hill, but it's all grown, all up through there now. The neighbors lived just through the woods from us. They always had raspberries and we would pick raspberries there in the spring and stuff. We'd all gather on the hill to play, over in the opening of the woods. In the wintertime we'd ski the hill in a barrel. We sure had some good times in those days. There was no drinking or dope or any of that stuff. But, even though I lived close to town, it wasn't a good relationship with the people in town. I was called dirty Indian and this and that several times by a lot of people. I mean, I always went to town school and I had white friends practically all my life, but there was still that name-calling by other people.

There was nine of us kids in the family and my mom was a dear. Yeah, she was a hard worker, she always worked out as a homemaker, a day worker in Belleville, in Napanee. She worked in Napanee for years in different households down there. When she worked in Napanee she stayed for the whole week down there, she was a live-in housekeeper. In Belleville, she just went for the day. She'd get a ride with different ones who worked that way. It got pretty lonesome when she worked in Napanee. But we all hauled in and did what we had to do. You had to do your part, that's just the way it was. When I went to Business College, my mother and father got scraping to put me through. I got a place in Belleville that I worked for my board and went to school in the day time. And I worked on Saturdays to make extra money for spending money. I stayed with some elderly lady in Belleville and she treated me very nice. We had to fare for ourselves when it came to education. But I know some people who just keep going to school, they don't work! They just want to be educated I guess.

I think, a long time ago, people cared more about each other. You visited more. Now, I mean, you daren't go to anybody's house unless you phone or you're invited. At home, we always had somebody there for our Sunday dinner. A relative or non-relative, they just came and we always put on extra plates for whoever came. I guess we're just not as friendly anymore. My house is wide open to anybody, if you want to come, come, because, I says, I'm usually there and you're more than welcome. A long time ago, everybody was friends, now you just have a few friends and have to be inviting and stuff like that. You never had to hire anybody to help with the thrashing, you'd just trade work. I know I've seen my mother cook for thirty men at hay time and thrashing time. Dad would kill a beef or a pig, and Mom would be making pies and puddings and hot biscuits. My mom fussed a lot over food. I'm not a fusser, just meat and potatoes and vegetable is my cooking. Mom would always be cooking, and she'd sew and bake and can to exhibit in the fair. She'd have to have everything just so, her peaches in a jar just so, and her pickles in a jar just so, and she could stand for hours and decorate things up, but not me!

Oh, I was always skating every chance I got. I got in more trouble for staying after school and playing, instead of home getting the cows! It was good fun because you didn't have to compete with the next guy, who had better clothes than you, or more money than you. We were all kind of happy-go-lucky, just glad to get together and have fun. You know, no drinking, or maybe they'd try to smoke, they used to sneak the odd smoke in. But I didn't start smoking until I was forty-three years old. I don't know why I started, now I think.

When I got to be a teenager, I was allowed to go to dances at the Council House with a date. During the war there was a restaurant in Deseronto where a bunch came out, there was a juke box and we danced, but I always had to be in by nine or ten o'clock. We had a radio at home, we played a lot of cards, I mean, it was more of a family type thing in those days. Like now, oh this one's gone that way, gone all skitter-scatter like. I wonder if they're really having fun. And in those days, when you had a friend, you had a friend! I don't know if everybody can say that now. The changes have happened at all the reserves. I mean, alcohol was one of the big problems. Still is, as far as I can see. But I always swore that I wouldn't be as poor as my mother and father was. That I was going to try and make something and save and have a little bit to fall back on, if need be. But I worry about things. I mean, there's no closeness, or community or unity. It seems like people just want to do for themselves, instead of the whole family.

I was always proud of being Mohawk, but I worked in the States when I was young, picking tomatoes in the fields on summer holidays. I never told them I was Mohawk. If somebody was to ask me if I was Italian, I would have said yes, you know, because it was safer. I worked the fields in the summer, staying with cousins at Tonawanda. I've always been proud of being Mohawk.

My husband was an electrician. He worked away a lot, he worked in Niagara Falls on the power plant there. He couldn't find work here, so he worked away a lot. I had the care of the children. We were building a house at the time, and at that time there was no money to be had, so we built our house from scratch. Yep, I got just as many nails in my house as my husband has, I guess! I pounded and pounded and pounded. That's what a marriage was. You both did your jobs. People today want everything at once, not like we started out, with a frying pan and a potato pot! People end up in debt and then you start fighting about money, then there goes the marriage. If you had a good marriage, you stayed committed to it.

I think the government interference has led to a lot of bad things. I mean, people started thinking that money was the answer to everything. It seems like if you do anything, you have to get paid for it. That's no way to raise children. I mean, money is nice, but it can't buy friends or pride.

I was twenty-four when I got married. We had a small wedding, my mother got supper for us, and we went to Niagara Falls for overnight and came home. I was working at the canning factory, and he was working. We rented a little cottage down on Bayshore Road, we had a hotplate and an icebox, a bed. And as I said, a frying pan and potato pot. We stayed there a little while, then he moved home, and I moved home. Not because we split up or anything, but to get ahead a little bit. Then he came home with me, and we started building our house. So, we built our house from scratch, and we had help. Mel Hill helped us. He was a carpenter then and he framed it. We didn't pay, he charged us a little bit, but we didn't pay him for years afterward! It seems like we were together every weekend. Mel and my husband were great pals, hunting and fishing together. And my husband trapped too. There was a fur-buyer in Napanee that would buy our fur. Yeah, him and Mel were great friends, all of us were.

I loved both of my parents. You're supposed to be close to your mother, but I think I was closer to my dad, really because he was with us more while Mother worked out. They were good parents. They tried their hardest to do for us. And I appreciate their hard work.

Earl Hill, 1928 –

I got most of my experience manually. I haven't got that great of education because I only went to public school. But I grew up and when I went out to work, I didn't go out to work to just make money. I went out to work to learn. And I worked on many different jobs. My dad used to give me the dickens because he said, why can't you hold a job? Well, I didn't want to hold a job, I wanted to learn how to do it and then I got out! So, that's the way I grew up and what I've learned on the outside, I've put to use since I became Chief. So, that's the way I got educated and I think it's a good way.

When I was a child and I found out that our people had nothing, I made up my mind that I would grow up and try to do something to help. So that's what I did. I got into politics and I've been in ever since. It's different now though. When I was a child, you could take everybody at their word. Now you can't. When I first got in Council, we had nothing and everybody was happy. But now, we've got a little bit and everybody wants it. Maybe too much greed and jealousy. That's not good. I've been Chief off and on for twenty years. I'll be glad to retire. (Chief Hill has since retired).

My father was an electrician. Mom stayed home and looked after the house. Dad drove back and forth. All the folks spoke Mohawk. But they didn't teach us because, as late as '68, we weren't allowed to talk it. It was against the law to talk your own language and try to promote it. I know some Mohawk, not all of it, I'm not fluent by no means, but my grandfather and grandmother talked to me all the time in Mohawk. I spent a lot of time with them, because I had a lot of chores at home and they told me a lot of different things. I don't know why, but I always catered to the older people. I guess 'cause they know the most. But I had a happy childhood. I listened to my relatives, I grew up with traditional culture. I was told stories and I tried to learn all I could. One time I was with my mother in the wagon. She was visiting some folks who had a death in the family. They lived out there where the airport is now. She was helping to lay the body out. When she came out to the wagon, she took the reins and started us out through the woods. The horse started bucking and making a terrible noise. Mother grabbed those reins tight and said, "It's just the ghost, don't be afraid." I covered my face with my hands while she plowed right through those woods, making that old horse go. I couldn't look. I think I didn't look until we were home. But all kinds of things like that happened. That's what I learned.

I've always been on the defensive about our people. And we gotta stay true to who we are. You can't back down. The more that is brought out, the better people respects it, 'cause you can't sit on a fence and say nothing. It's the grassroots that get things done. In the old days, when we had an Indian agent, they was always trying to push things down our throat. Making our decisions for us. That's no way to live. But we finally got rid of them.

I've never run across another Territory that operates like we do. We don't have the degree of poverty that most reserves have. Now, we're not prosperous, but we take care of our own. And there was poverty and alcohol troubles at one time. I blame the government. The welfare programs just weren't good for us. It made us too dependent on them. Too many people were raised that didn't have to work. And being Native, the white society labels Indians as lazy drunkards, and we can't let them make us believe that's true. There were times I couldn't get a job 'cause I was Native. But I always found something else to do. I was a carpenter, a cleaner, a maintenance man, I worked as a truck driver. I was farming, I was making bricks, I learned how to do all kinds of things. You don't get rich, but it's good work and the government can't take that away, that good feeling of working.

I'm moving on to my next challenge, starting a restaurant. And then I've got my garden. I've always liked gardening. It's too bad that folks don't garden as much as they used to. You don't starve!

I've had an interesting life. If I had it to do over, I wouldn't change many things. Maybe a few! But I had a vision when I was younger, about being Chief and helping out the people. I tried to do my best. You know, this is the Mother Reserve of the Iroquois Confederacy, and it's very special here. All of us have to do our part.

Freda Baptiste, 1929 –

I went up to grade eight and stayed there for three years until I was fifteen, and then I quit and went to work. I used to hitch-hike to Belleville and I worked in the Chinese laundry. I ironed white shirts all day. I think I'd get about sixty-five cents. The bus was thirteen cents, but I used to hitch-hike, eh. But hitch-hiking in them days wasn't like it is nowadays, you know.

I was born down the highway there, before you get to Milltown. There used to be a school in Milltown, so we could walk there. There was two more Indian families that lived there. It was hard going to a white school alone, when you were Indian, then. They think the kids now, they've got it hard being an Indian and going to a high school. They don't know what hard is! I used to get a lickin' every day. I was smart and I liked to learn, yet today, I've never gone back to school. Most of the teachers, and especially the principal, they were white eh, and they just didn't like Indians. Indian kids. Indian period! It was hard, it was hard going. I never went to an Indian school. We had it hard. I'm writing a book, and when I finish it, I'm not publishing it until after I'm dead. I'm going to leave it in my will to somebody. It'll make them rich, eh? 'Cause nobody will believe it anyway. No. Our life has been hard, my life especially.

My father done absolutely nothing but drink and run around and then come home and make kids for my mother. He had sixteen, he went and had sixteen kids. Four died, she lost four, like in them days

Freda Baptiste

you had them at home, eh, and you never knew why they died. Four, they was all girls. She got married when she was twenty-two and she lost the last kid when she was forty-four. In twenty-two years she had sixteen kids. Then my father sent four of the kids away to the Christian Mohawk Home in Sault Ste. Marie. I didn't know them though. I wasn't born when they was sent away. Oh, I guess my mother never said anything. Whatever my father did was....I don't understand, I don't understand that. But when I got married, I lived the same way. For a long while. I didn't know any different either. I just started having kids, and you don't know that you don't have to, or that you're supposed to open up your mouth and speak once in a while. I know now!

Yeah, my father used to beat my mother. She was always scared of him. Always. We were all scared. I was scared of him even when I was married and living in this house and had all my kids. I was still deathly scared of my father. When I lived home, I'd hide under the bed. I had nightmares every night for three years. My mother had to get up when he got home drunk, cook him something to eat, eh. One time, I remember one time, she wasn't going to get up. He throwed her and the bed downstairs. She got on up, she fell out of the bed, went and cooked him something to eat. Yeah, we had it bad. He never worked. Then he went to the States, he got a job over there. Once in a while he'd come home. Most of the time he didn't. We had just what my mother could get us, eh, which wasn't much. We had a little garden, a nice garden. But my father sold off our land and took the money and went off and never came back until the money was gone. We had acres and acres of strawberries, and tomatoes. I don't know what it's like to have a father. You know, I can't remember ever going near my father. We were all like that.

I never had fun as a kid. I can never remember playing with anybody when I was little. Not even at school because they were all white kids, eh. They were programmed that Indian is bad. And we'd go to school with no shoes on, eh, and we'd have no lunch. Just a big hard bun for bread, eh, and they would make fun of that, and think we were different, because we didn't have the things they had. We could've if my father would have worked. Like I didn't bring my kids up like that. No. We had it hard too, when my kids were small. Wages weren't all that good then, but I can't remember my kids going to school with no shoes or just a scone for lunch. I always made sure they ate. But of course, John worked and kept us going, like men are supposed to do. My father must have thought he was different. Oh, after we grew up he worked. In the States at those big huge paper mills. Sometimes my mother would take us and live over there with him. Forget it! He never kept us any better over there than he did at home. He just spent all the money on women and booze. And we lived on welfare, on Red Cross and all that other crap.

So, I started work when I was fifteen, then I went to the States and got a job over there. After we was married, John and me and the kids lived in Buffalo. It was a big city. It's a hard city to live in, especially when you're just poor and getting along, you know. We stayed over there for three years with John and he worked in the Falls. I couldn't stand it any longer. Cars would squeak their brakes and I would run way outside and here my kids are sitting in the house! Yeah, I was a nervous wreck over there. Not after living in the country, you know, all your life, bringing your kids up, then move to Buffalo! Oh!

See, way back then, it wasn't so much Indian, Indian then. We didn't know of any community. Even over there we were looked down on because we were Indian, eh. Now, there's an Indian place you can go to and this and that. But it wasn't like that then. The other people would say we were dirty Indians and lazy Indians. But I always used to stand up for myself because I wasn't dirty and I wasn't lazy. I always spoke up for myself because I liked being Indian. And I'll always be proud I'm Indian. Nobody will ever take that away from me. Sometimes I sit and wonder why, though. We've had it so hard eh? I guess it was just born in me to be proud. It's my nationality, you know. Like one day my daughter-in-law and me was talking here, and she said, "Freda, do you wish that Mario would have married Indian instead of me?" And I said, "Well, certainly I do, you know." Any mother wants her sons to marry their own nationality. My youngest son, he married white too. But, I didn't tell him who to fall in love with, you know. Nobody told me who, and me, maybe I'd have been better off if I would've fell in love with a white man instead of an Indian. But I don't know that. I never looked down on my daughter-in-laws because they're not Indian. I wish they would've been Indian, but they're good to my sons, they make good wives.

My mother and father always spoke Mohawk, but when we were inside the house they spoke English. When I was little, when they didn't want us to know what they were saying, they talked Indian. I wish they would've talked it to me. We always know when they didn't want us to know, and I would have liked to learn to talk in my own language, eh. And I like to sing Mohawk too. They have Mohawk Singers, but I never joined. I think because of the way I grew up. Always made to stay by ourselves, eh, don't go here, don't go there. I can never remember playing with another kid. Only my brothers and sisters. And I think that's why I'm not a joiner. Oh, I'll help anybody that asks. But we went to a white school, and I never got to know the other people my age. I never went to school with them, and then we moved to the States, and then we'd move home, then we'd move back to the States, and we were never around the Indians here. I miss that.

Me and John were married here. His father and mother owned this big house on the York Road. John's father was a Mohawk language teacher, and John can't talk Mohawk either! His mother didn't know it, so they talked English in the house. Way back, when my mother and father got married, my father couldn't read or write, but my mother taught him to. That's why I wonder why my parents didn't teach us the language. But, like I said, back then the people weren't so proud to be Indian. I was always Indian as long as I can remember and I brought up my kids that way, even my grandson is proud to be Indian.

We struggled along. When I had kids we lived at John's mother and father's place because we never had electric, or we never had running water, and I washed on a wash board, hung my clothes out to dry. My kids were brought up good, though. They were never sick. I always gave them good food, you know. I always gave them vitamins, and we never had big bunches of money or big bunches of food, but I always made sure they got what they were supposed to get. And he was a good provider for them, John, he was. I suppose that had a lot to do with it, because my father never provided anything. I could remember us, once I can remember going to bed three days in a row, and nothing to eat at all. Getting up and nothing to eat, going to bed and nothing to eat, getting up and nothing to eat, and my mother was sick in bed, getting another baby. But I never brought mine up like that, you know. They never had everything they wanted, but they had what they really needed.

My grandson, he's eight and he learns the language in school and comes here and we can discuss Indian problems. Eight years old! He's fair and he gets sunburned, and he's got red hair, but the Indian is there inside. In his soul he's Mohawk and nobody can take your soul, no. That's what we have, our soul. And my other grandchild, she went to school the first time this year, kindergarten. She came up to the house and said, "I come up to sing for you, Grandma." I said, "What did you learn?" "I learned an Indian song." She's standing there singing away, and she put her head down like this, and I said, "When you're singing Mohawk, you put your head right up in the air and you look right at the people, don't ever put your head down." So she stands there just singing, and I don't even know what it means! She's talking Mohawk and her mother's English, right straight from England! The baby can say different words in Mohawk and she's so proud. I am too.

John always worked away. He was a mine worker and had to go where the work was. So, I had the total responsibility of the kids for most of their life. But I don't regret staying home with them. I got to know them and that's a good thing. When John was forty-four, he fell at work, he broke every bone in his body. Every bone. He was all done in traction, everything was in a cast, eh, but his mouth. And his face was starting to droop, big, but he wanted a smoke though. He's a smoker, eh, he wanted a smoke so bad. So we moved the bed out there where there wasn't any oxygen, and I gave him a smoke!

My kids took care of everything when that happened. My daughter was only sixteen and she made sure the young ones went to school. Compensation was only seventy dollars a week, and that had to go in the bank to make the car payments. See, we used to get a new car pretty often because John used to drive back and forth to work. He'd work in Washington, then he'd work in Pennsylvania, then he'd work in Rochester, he'd work all over, eh. So he always had to have a good car. But we had just bought a new car before he fell. So that money went in the bank to make payments. We never had life insurance or sickness. I think he was four months in Rochester and I had to stay over there. My oldest son used to bring the kids on the weekends. Either that or he'd come and get me and I'd come home for a couple of days. They wanted me to put John in a rehabilitation hospital because he was all in a cast. They told me we couldn't look after him at home, but we did. I had him home for nine months, then his cast got too small. We fed him too good! His cast was squeezing him. He was supposed to keep the cast on for a year, eh, but it got taken off in nine months.

He's got a quarter inch missing from his leg. They wanted to take five inches off his leg. And I told them, no. And I prayed. I said it will be all right, just tend to the other things and I'll pray. And four months went by and the bone that was powdered just grew back again. I said to them doctors, now see, I told you. I burnt tobacco and prayed, but I had no doubt that it would be alright. John has died many times, but then he come back to life, eh. He's good, he's strong, he gets up, he drives the tractor, we go to the woods. He can't work anymore, but he gets around. Everybody thought he would die for good but I knew he wouldn't. Some say I'm a witch. It taught me a lot of things, this being sick and him being sick, and the kids, the kids dying. You don't give up that faith when you're Indian, eh.

There was a time when I couldn't pray, so much death and mourning. I didn't believe anymore, I was just mad at everything. Mad at the sun for shining! But, I got better. Everybody takes their own time to heal. My son died, my grandson died, but I had to get up and live every day. I sometimes think if I was a different nationality I'd have cracked up long ago! But Indians are good and strong, you know. Indian people are good people and strong people. Oh, there's a lot of bad Indians, bad people. But they're not really Indians. They forgot what being an Indian means. We've had it rough, me and

John, but we've come through it alright. When you go to bed, you never know what's going to take place the next day, you know, you just be thankful that you're in your own bed and everything's all right at that time.

We never asked anybody for anything. John was always real independent. Me too. If we can't do it ourselves then we don't need it. Some people run to the government for this and for that. It's better if you work towards something. We rely on the government for too much. Now I'm not saying that the government don't owe us for all the heartache we've been through. Education is important. Our language is important. But we can't be self-sufficient if the government has to bail us out of mistakes we make. We learn lessons from mistakes. We're Indian. We don't need whites to tell us what to do.

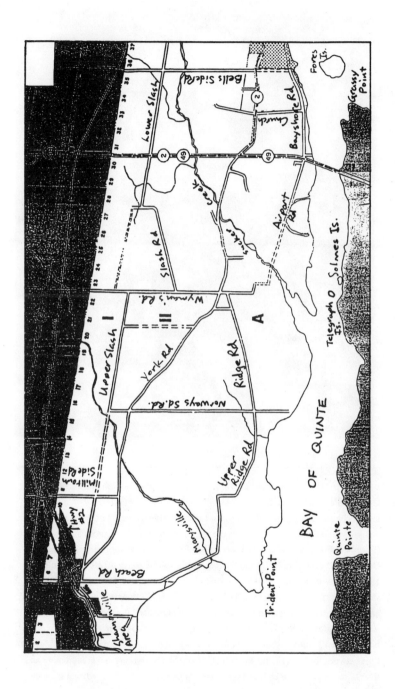

119 ~

BETH BRANT is a Bay of Quinte Mohawk from Tyendinaga Mohawk Territory in Ontario. She was born on May 6, 1941. She is the editor of *A Gathering of Spirit*, the ground-breaking collection of writing and art by Native women (Firebrand Books, USA and Women's Press, Canada). She is the author of *Mohawk Trail*, prose and poetry (Firebrand Books and Women's Press, 1985) *Food & Spirits*, short fiction (Firebrand Books and Press Gang, 1991) and *Writing as Witness: Essay and Talk* (Women's Press, 1994). Her work has appeared in numerous Native, feminist and lesbian anthologies and she has done readings, lectures and taught throughout North America. She has received an Ontario Arts Council award, a Canada Council grant and is a recipient of a National Endowment for the Arts Literature Fellowship. Beth Brant is currently working on a book entitled *Testimony from the Faithful*, essays about land and spirit. She divides her time between living in Michigan and in Canada. She is a mother and grandmother and lives with her partner of eighteen years, Denise Dorsz. She has been writing since the age of forty and considers it a gift for her community.